Knit your own
Dinosaur

First published in the United Kingdom in 2015
by
Pavilion
1 Gower Street
London
WC1E 6HD

ISBN 9781910496428

A CIP catalogue record for this book is
available from the British Library.

10 9 8 7 6 5 4 3 2 1

Photography by Holly Jolliffe

Reproduction by Tag Publishing, UK
Printed and bound by GPS, Slovenia

This book can be ordered direct from the
publisher at www.pavilionbooks.com

For Geoffrey, Abigail, Gabriel, Orlando, Daniel and Milo.

Knit your own
Dinosaur

Sally Muir & Joanna Osborne

PAVILION

Contents

Introduction

Knit your own Dinosaur is the latest addition to our *Best in Show* series, and the first to feature animals that are no longer with us. As nobody knows for sure what colour dinosaurs were, it has given us licence to be a little more adventurous with our colours, and so can you. We hope that we have chosen a representative selection for you, with a variety of shapes and sizes, from the winged to the crawling, from the long-necked to the squat and menacing.

We have added armature wire as well as pipecleaners to help strengthen our dinosaurs and make them more poseable. As before, the dinosaurs are not toys, but the ends of armature wire are less sharp than those of pipecleaners, so may be better for small children. Or you can stuff the dinosaurs very tightly and not use anything, if you don't mind them being slightly floppy.

Although none of them is particularly difficult to knit, if you are a more inexperienced knitter we would advise beginning with the simpler dinosaurs: the Brachiosaurus, Diplodocus, Archelon, Pterodactyl, Mammoth, Stegosaurus and Tyrannosaurus Rex. When you are more confident, you can proceed to the slightly more complicated Velociraptor, Archaeopteryx, Iguanodon, Triceratops and Ankylosaurus.

We do hope that you enjoy knitting our dinosaurs as much as we have enjoyed creating them.

Joanna and Sally

Diplodocus

A beautifully balanced creature, the Diplodocus is one of the longest of the known dinosaurs. Because of its long neck, the Diplodocus had a vast heart in order to breathe, and used its long tail as a whip to deter predators. For years, 'Dippy', a Diplodocus fossil, has greeted visitors in the entrance hall of the Natural History Museum in London.

Diplodocus

This is one of the simplest dinosaurs to knit, but perhaps a little more tricky to put together.

Measurements
Length: 55cm (21½in)
Height to centre back: 17cm (6¾in)

Materials
Pair of 3¾mm (US 5) knitting needles
Double-pointed 3¾mm (US 5) knitting needles (for holding stitches)
50g (2oz) of Rowan Pure Wool Worsted in Hazel 128 (hz)
30g (1¼oz) of Rowan Pure Wool Worsted in Hawthorn 141 (ha)
Small amount of Rowan Felted Tweed in Ginger 154 (gn)
2 small black beads for eyes and sewing needle and black thread for sewing on
57cm (22½in) of 2mm armature wire for head, body and tail
2 pipecleaners for legs

Abbreviations
See page 78.
See page 79 for Colour Knitting.

Right Back Leg
With hz, cast on 15 sts.
Beg with a k row, work 2 rows st st.
Row 3: Inc, k4, k2tog, k1, k2tog, k4, inc. (15 sts)
Row 4: Purl.
Rep rows 3–4 once more.
Row 7: K2tog, k11, k2tog. (13 sts)
Work 7 rows st st.
Row 15: K5, inc, k1, inc, k5. (15 sts)
Work 3 rows st st.
Row 19: K6, inc, k1, inc, k6. (17 sts)
Row 20: Purl.
Row 21: Inc, k6, inc, k1, inc, k6, inc. (21 sts)
Work 3 rows st st.*
Join in ha.
Row 25: K9hz, inchz, k1ha, incha, k9hz. (23 sts)
Row 26: P8hz, p4ha, p11hz.
Row 27: K11hz, k5ha, k7hz.
Row 28: P5hz, p7ha, p11hz.
Row 29: Cast (bind) off 11hz sts, k1hz icos, k7ha, k4hz (hold 12 sts on spare needle for Right Side of Body).

Left Back Leg
Work as for Right Back Leg to *.
Join in ha.
Row 25: K9hz, incha, k1ha, inchz, k9hz. (23 sts)
Row 26: P11hz, k4ha, p8hz.
Row 27: K7hz, k5ha, k11hz.
Row 28: P11hz, p7ha, p5hz.
Row 29: K4hz, k8ha, cast (bind) off 11hz sts (hold 12 sts on spare needle for Left Side of Body).

Right Front Leg
With hz, cast on 13 sts.
Beg with a k row, work 2 rows st st.
Row 3: Inc, k3, k2tog, k1, k2tog, k3, inc. (13 sts)
Row 4: Purl.
Rep rows 3–4 once more.

Row 7: K2tog, k9, k2tog. (11 sts)
Work 5 rows st st.
Row 13: K4, inc, k1, inc, k4. (13 sts)
Work 5 rows st st.
Row 19: K5, inc, k1, inc, k5. (15 sts)
Work 2 rows st st.**
Join in ha.
Row 22: P7hz, p2ha, p6hz.
Row 23: Inchz, k5hz, k4ha, k4hz, inchz. (17 sts)
Row 24: P5hz, p5ha, p7hz.
Row 25: Cast (bind) off 8hz sts, k1hz icos, k5ha, k3hz (hold 9 sts on spare needle for Right Side of Body and Head).

Left Front Leg
Work as for Right Front Leg to **.
Join in ha.
Row 22: P6hz, p2ha, p7hz.
Row 23: Inchz, k4hz, k4ha, k5hz, inchz. (17 sts)
Row 24: P7hz, p5ha, p5hz.
Row 25: K3hz, k6ha, cast (bind) off 8hz sts (hold 9 sts on spare needle for Left Side of Body and Head).

Right Side of Body and Head
Row 1: With ha, cast on 2 sts, with RS facing k9 from spare needle of Right Front Leg, cast on 8 sts. (19 sts)
Row 2: Purl.
Row 3: Inc, k18, cast on 7 sts, with RS facing p1, k11 from spare needle of Right Back Leg, cast on 50 sts. (89 sts)
Row 4: Cast (bind) off 12 sts, p49 icos, k1, p27, cast on 18 sts. (95 sts)
Row 5: Inc, k44, p1, k47, k2tog. (95 sts)
Row 6: Cast (bind) off 7 sts, p41 icos, k1, p46, cast on 12 sts. (100 sts)
Row 7: Inc, k57, p1, k39, k2tog. (100 sts)
Row 8: Cast (bind) off 6 sts, p34 icos, k1, p59, cast on 8 sts. (102 sts)
Row 9: K68, p1, k31, k2tog. (101 sts)
Row 10: Cast (bind) off 5 sts, p27 icos, k1,

p33, cast (bind) off 28 sts, p to end. (61 sts and 7 sts)

Row 11: Working on 7 sts for head only, knit.

Row 12: P5, p2tog. (6 sts)

Row 13: K2tog, k2, k2tog. (4 sts) Cast (bind) off.

Row 14: Rejoin ha to rem 61 sts, k2tog, k32, p1, k24, k2tog. (59 sts)

Row 15: Cast (bind) off 4 sts, p20 icos, k1, p32, p2tog. (54 sts)

Row 16: Cast (bind) off 2 sts, k32 icos, p1, k17, k2tog. (51 sts)

Row 17: Cast (bind) off 4 sts, p12 icos, k2, p31, p2tog. (46 sts)

Row 18: Cast (bind) off 4 sts, k40 icos, k2tog. (41 sts)

Row 19: Cast (bind) off 3 sts, p36 icos, p2tog. (37 sts)

Row 20: Cast (bind) off 6 sts, k29 icos, k2tog. (30 sts)

Row 21: Cast (bind) off 4 sts, p24 icos, p2tog. (25 sts)

Row 22: Cast (bind) off 4 sts, k19 icos, k2tog. (20 sts)

Row 23: Cast (bind) off 2 sts, p16 icos, p2tog. (17 sts)

Row 24: Cast (bind) off 2 sts, k13 icos, k2tog. (14 sts)

Row 25: Cast (bind) off 2 sts, p10 icos, p2tog. (11 sts)

Row 26: K2tog, k7, k2tog. (9 sts) Cast (bind) off.

Legs and spine

Use pipecleaners to stiffen the legs and armature wire to act as a spine running through the body. Armature wire is very easy to manipulate and holds up the head and tail.

Left Side of Body and Head

Row 1: With ha, cast on 2 sts, with WS facing p9 from spare needle of Left Front Leg, cast on 8 sts. (19 sts)

Row 2: Knit.

Row 3: Inc, p18, cast on 7 sts, with WS facing k1, p11 from spare needle of Left Back Leg, cast on 50 sts. (89 sts)

Row 4: Cast (bind) off 12 sts, k49 icos, p1, k27, cast on 18 sts. (95 sts)

Row 5: Inc, p44, k1, p47, p2tog. (95 sts)

Row 6: Cast (bind) off 7 sts, k41 icos, p1, k46, cast on 12 sts. (100 sts)

Row 7: Inc, p57, k1, p39, p2tog. (100 sts)

Row 8: Cast (bind) off 6 sts, k34 icos, p1, k59, cast on 8 sts. (102 sts)

Row 9: P68, k1, p31, p2tog. (101 sts)

Row 10: Cast (bind) off 5 sts, k27 icos, p1, k33, cast (bind) off 28 sts, k to end. (61 sts and 7 sts)

Row 11: Working on 7 sts only for head, purl.

Row 12: K5, k2tog. (6 sts)

Row 13: P2tog, p2, p2tog. (4 sts)

Cast (bind) off.

Row 14: Rejoin ha to rem 61 sts, p2tog, p32, k1, p24, p2tog. (59 sts)

Row 15: Cast (bind) off 4 sts, k20 icos, p1, k32, k2tog. (54 sts)

Row 16: Cast (bind) off 2 sts, p32 icos, k1, p17, p2tog. (51 sts)

Row 17: Cast (bind) off 4 sts, k12 icos, p2, k31, k2tog. (46 sts)

Row 18: Cast (bind) off 4 sts, p40 icos, p2tog. (41 sts)

Row 19: Cast (bind) off 3 sts, k36 icos, k2tog. (37 sts)

Row 20: Cast (bind) off 6 sts, p29 icos, p2tog. (30 sts)

Row 21: Cast (bind) off 4 sts, k24 icos, k2tog. (25 sts)

Row 22: Cast (bind) off 4 sts, p19 icos, p2tog. (20 sts)

Row 23: Cast (bind) off 2 sts, k16 icos, k2tog. (17 sts)

Row 24: Cast (bind) off 2 sts, p13 icos, p2tog. (14 sts)

Row 25: Cast (bind) off 2 sts, k10 icos, k2tog. (11 sts)

Row 26: P2tog, p7, p2tog. (9 sts)

Cast (bind) off.

Tummy

With hz, cast on 2 sts.

Row 1: [Inc] twice. (4 sts)

Row 2: Purl.

Row 3: K1, [inc] twice, k1. (6 sts)

Row 4: Purl.

Row 5: K2, [inc] twice, k2. (8 sts)

Row 6: Purl.

Row 7: K3, [inc] twice, k3. (10 sts)

Work 3 rows st st.

Row 11: K2tog, k6, k2tog. (8 sts)

Row 12: P2tog, p4, p2tog. (6 sts)

Row 13: K2, [inc] twice, k2. (8 sts)

Work 9 rows st st.

Row 23: Inc, k6, inc. (10 sts)

Row 24: Inc, p3, inc, p4, inc. (13 sts)

Row 25: K6, p1, k6.

Row 26: P6, k1, p6.

Rep rows 25–26 once more.

Row 29: K5, inc, p1, inc, k5. (15 sts)

Row 30: P7, k1, p7.

Row 31: K7, p1, k7.

Rep rows 30–31, 7 times more.

Row 46: P7, k1, p7.

Row 47: K2tog, k5, p1, k5, k2tog. (13 sts)

Row 48: P2tog, p4, k1, p4, p2tog. (11 sts)

Row 49: K3, k2tog, p1, k2tog, k3. (9 sts)

Row 50: P4, k1, p4.

Row 51: K4, p1, k4.

Rep rows 50–51 twice more.

Row 56: P4, k1, p4.

Row 57: K2, k2tog, p1, k2tog, k2. (7 sts)

Row 58: P3, k1, p3.

Row 59: K1, k2tog, p1, k2tog, k1. (5 sts)

Row 60: P2, k1, p2.

Row 61: K2, p1, k2.

Rep rows 60–61 once more.
Row 64: P2tog, p1, p2tog. (3 sts)
Row 65: K3tog and fasten off.

To Make Up

SEWING IN ENDS Sew in ends, leaving ends from cast on and cast (bound) off rows for sewing up.

LEGS With WS together, fold each leg in half and sew up on RS, starting at feet.

HEAD AND BODY With WS together and starting 3cm (1¼in) from front of front legs, sew around head, along back and around tail to 2.5cm (1in) from back of back leg. Using pliers, fold over 2.5cm (1in) at each end of the armature wire. Insert wire into the tail, up through body along spine and up the neck into the head. The wire hangs loose within the main body.

TUMMY With RS of body and WS of tummy (reverse st st side) together, sew cast on row of tummy to top of tail, and sew cast (bound) off row to front of front legs. Ease and sew tummy to fit body, leaving a 2.5cm (1in) gap between front and back legs on one side.

STUFFING Pipecleaners are used to stiffen the legs and help bend them into shape. Fold a pipecleaner into a 'U' shape and measure against front two legs. Cut to approximately fit, leaving an extra 2.5cm (1in) at both ends. Fold over the ends. Roll a little stuffing around pipecleaner and slip into body, one end down each front leg. Repeat with second pipecleaner and back legs. Starting at the head, stuff the Diplodocus firmly, using the end of a knitting needle to ease the stuffing into tail and neck, then sew up the gap. Mould body into shape.

SPINES With gn, make approx 22 2-loop French knots, about 1cm (½in) apart, along the spine.

EYES Sew on black beads positioned as in photograph.

Tyrannosaurus Rex

King of the dinosaurs as well as a legendary 1970s glam rock band, the Tyrannosaurus Rex was one of the largest carnivorous dinosaurs, able to eat up to 500 pounds of meat in one bite. It also had very bad breath and a septic bite. Its tiny little arms have caused some hilarity, but may have been used for grasping prey or pushing itself up if it fell over. T-Rex the band became popular with hits such as 'Ride A White Swan' and 'Get It On', but the band became extinct when lead singer Marc Bolan died in 1977.

Tyrannosaurus Rex

The T-Rex is the largest dinosaur to make, but has a wire spine to help him stand up.

Measurements
Length: 31cm (12¼in)
Height to top of head: 34cm (13½in)

Materials
Pair of 3¾mm (US 5) knitting needles
Double-pointed 3¾mm (US 5) knitting
    needles (for holding stitches)
20g (¾oz) of Rowan Felted Tweed Aran in
    Dusty 728 (du)
75g (2¾oz) of Rowan Felted Tweed Aran in
    Garden 740 (ga)
5g (⅛oz) of Rowan Felted Tweed in Paisley
    171 (pa)
Small amount of Rowan Pure Wool DK in
    Enamel 013 (en) for teeth
Tiny amount of Rowan Pure Wool DK in
    Black 004 (bl) for eyes
2 tiny yellow or gold beads for eyes and
    sewing needle and yellow thread for
    sewing on
120cm (48in) of 2mm armature wire for
    head, body, back legs, and tail
1 pipecleaner for front legs

Abbreviations
See page 78.
See page 79 for Wrap and Turn Method.

Right Back Leg
Claws
With du, cast on 1 st and work in garter st.

Row 1: Knit.
Row 2: Inc. (2 sts)
Change to ga.
Row 3: [Inc] twice. (4 sts)
Beg with a p row, work 5 rows st st (hold
4 sts on spare needle for working foot).
Rep from beg twice more, leaving third
Claw on main needle. (8 sts on spare
needle in total)
Shape foot
Row 9: With RS facing, k4 from third Claw,
then k8 from spare needle of first two Claws.
(12 sts)
Row 10: P2tog, p8, p2tog. (10 sts)
Work 4 rows st st.
Row 15: K2tog, k6, k2tog. (8 sts)
Work 5 rows st st.
Row 21: K2tog, k4, k2tog. (6 sts)
Work 5 rows st st.
Row 27: K1, inc, k2, inc, k1. (8 sts)
Work 5 rows st st.
Row 33: K1, inc, k4, inc, k1. (10 sts)
Work 3 rows st st.
Row 37: K1, inc, k6, inc, k1. (12 sts)
Work 3 rows st st.
Row 41: K1, inc, k8, inc, k1. (14 sts)
Work 3 rows st st.
Row 45: K1, inc, k10, inc, k1. (16 sts)
Work 3 rows st st.
Row 49: K1, [k2tog, k2] 3 times, k2tog, k1.
(12 sts)
Row 50: Purl.
Row 51: K1, [inc, k2] 3 times, inc, k1. (16 sts)
Row 52: Purl.
Row 53: K1, inc, k12, inc, k1. (18 sts)
Work 3 rows st st.
Row 57: K1, [inc, k4] 3 times, inc, k1. (22 sts)
Work 3 rows st st.
Row 61: K1, inc, k18, inc, k1. (24 sts)
Work 3 rows st st.*
Row 65: Cast (bind) off 12 sts, k to end
(hold 12 sts on spare needle for Right Side
of Body).

Left Back Leg
Work as Right Back Leg to *.
Row 65: K12, cast (bind) off 12 sts (hold
12 sts on spare needle for Left Side of Body).

Front Legs
(make 2 the same)
With ga, cast on 6 sts.
Beg with a k row, work 4 rows st st.
Row 5: K1, [k2tog] twice, k1. (4 sts)
Work 11 rows st st.
Row 17: K2tog, turn.
Row 18: Working on 1 st only, purl.
Row 19: Knit.
Fasten off.
Row 20: Rejoin yarn, k2tog, turn.
Row 21: Working on 1 st only, purl.
Row 22: Knit.
Fasten off.

Right Side of Body
With ga, cast on 50 sts.
Row 1: Cast (bind) off 10 sts, p40 icos, with
WS facing p12 from spare needle of Right
Back Leg, cast on 2 sts. (54 sts)
Row 2: K13, p1, k40.
Row 3: Cast (bind) off 8 sts, p32 icos, k1,
p13, cast on 2 sts. (48 sts)
Row 4: K14, p1, k31, k2tog. (47 sts)
Row 5: Cast (bind) off 6 sts, p26 icos, k1,
p13, inc. (42 sts)
Row 6: K16, p1, k23, k2tog. (41 sts)
Row 7: Cast (bind) off 6 sts, p18 icos, k1,
p15, inc. (36 sts)
Row 8: K17, p1, k16, k2tog. (35 sts)
Row 9: Cast (bind) off 4 sts, p12 icos, k1,
p17, inc. (32 sts)
Row 10: K19, p1, k12.
Row 11: Cast (bind) off 4 sts, p8 icos, k1,
p18, inc. (29 sts)
Row 12: K20, p1, k8.
Row 13: P2tog, p7, k1, p18, inc.
Row 14: K20, p1, k8.
Row 15: P2tog, p26, inc.

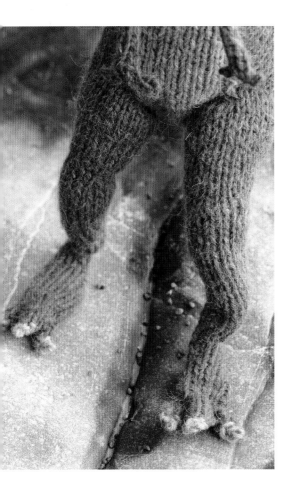

Feet

As with the real thing, the three-toed feet and tail form a tripod.

Row 16: Knit.
Row 17: P2tog, p26, inc.
Row 18: Knit.
Row 19: P2tog, p26, inc.
Row 20: Knit.
Row 21: Cast (bind) off 3 sts, p25 icos, inc. (27 sts)
Row 22: Knit.
Row 23: Cast (bind) off 3 sts, p23 icos, inc. (25 sts)
Row 24: Knit.
Row 25: Cast (bind) off 4 sts, p20 icos, inc. (22 sts)
Row 26: Knit.
Row 27: Cast (bind) off 4 sts, p17 icos, inc. (19 sts)
Row 28: Knit.
Row 29: Cast (bind) off 6 sts, p12 icos, inc. (14 sts)
Row 30: Knit.
Row 31: Cast (bind) off 3 sts, p10 icos, inc (hold 12 sts on spare needle for Neck and Head).

Left Side of Body
With ga, cast on 50 sts.
Row 1: Cast (bind) off 10 sts, k40 icos, with RS facing k12 from spare needle of Left Back Leg, cast on 2 sts. (54 sts)
Row 2: P13, k1, p40.
Row 3: Cast (bind) off 8 sts, k32 icos, p1, k13, cast on 2 sts. (48 sts)
Row 4: P14, k1, p31, p2tog. (47 sts)
Row 5: Cast (bind) off 6 sts, k26 icos, p1, k13, inc. (42 sts)
Row 6: P16, k1, p23, p2tog. (41 sts)
Row 7: Cast (bind) off 6 sts, k18 icos, p1, k15, inc. (36 sts)
Row 8: P17, k1, p16, p2tog. (35 sts)
Row 9: Cast (bind) off 4 sts, k12 icos, p1, k17, inc. (32 sts)
Row 10: P19, k1, p12.
Row 11: Cast (bind) off 4 sts, k8 icos, p1, k18, inc. (29 sts)

Row 12: P20, k1, p8.
Row 13: K2tog, k7, p1, k18, inc.
Row 14: P20, k1, p8.
Row 15: K2tog, k26, inc.
Row 16: Purl.
Row 17: K2tog, k26, inc.
Row 18: Purl.
Row 19: K2tog, k26, inc.
Row 20: Purl.
Row 21: Cast (bind) off 3 sts, k25 icos, inc. (27 sts)
Row 22: Purl.
Row 23: Cast (bind) off 3 sts, k23 icos, inc. (25 sts)
Row 24: Purl.
Row 25: Cast (bind) off 4 sts, k20 icos, inc. (22 sts)
Row 26: Purl.
Row 27: Cast (bind) off 4 sts, k17 icos, inc. (19 sts)
Row 28: Purl.
Row 29: Cast (bind) off 6 sts, k12 icos, inc. (14 sts)
Row 30: Purl.
Row 31: Cast (bind) off 3 sts, k10 icos, inc (hold 12 sts on spare needle for Neck and Head).

Neck and Head
Row 1: With ga, with RS facing k12 from spare needle of Right Side of Body, then k12 from spare needle of Left Side of Body. (24 sts)
Row 2: Purl.
Row 3: K1, [k2tog, k8] twice, k2tog, k1. (21 sts)
Row 4: Purl.
Row 5: K1, k2tog, k15, k2tog, k1. (19 sts)
Row 6: Purl.
Row 7: K1, k2tog, k13, k2tog, k1. (17 sts)
Row 8: Purl.
Row 9: [K1, inc] twice, k2, inc, k3, inc, k2, [inc, k1] twice. (23 sts)
Row 10: Inc, p21, inc. (25 sts)

Row 11: K20, w&t (leave 5 sts on left-hand needle unworked).
Row 12: Working on centre 15 sts only, p15, w&t.
Row 13: K15, w&t.
Row 14: P15, w&t.
Rep rows 13-14 twice more.
Row 19: K20. (25 sts in total)
Row 20: P1, p2tog, p19, p2tog, p1. (23 sts)
Row 21: K1, k2tog, k17, k2tog, k1. (21 sts)
Row 22: Purl.
Row 23: K1, k2tog, k15, k2tog, k1. (19 sts)
Row 24: Purl.
Row 25: K15, w&t (leave 4 sts on left-hand needle unworked).
Row 26: Working on centre 11 sts only, p11, w&t.
Row 27: K11, w&t.
Row 28: P11, w&t.
Rep rows 27-28 twice more.
Row 33: K15. (19 sts in total)
Row 34: Purl.
Row 35: [K1, k2tog] twice, k7, [k2tog, k1] twice. (15 sts)
Row 36: Purl.
Row 37: K1, k2tog, k9, k2tog, k1. (13 sts)
Row 38: Purl.
Row 39: K1, k2tog, k7, k2tog, k1. (11 sts)
Work 3 rows st st.
Row 43: K2tog, k5, k2tog, k1. (9 sts)
Row 44: P1, p2tog, p3, p2tog, p1. (7 sts)
Cast (bind) off.

Tummy
With du, cast on 2 sts.
Row 1: Knit.
Row 2: Purl.
Row 3: [Inc] twice. (4 sts)
Row 4: Purl.
Row 5: Inc, k2, inc. (6 sts)
Row 6: Purl.
Row 7: Inc, k4, inc. (8 sts)
Row 8: Purl.
Row 9: Inc, k6, inc. (10 sts)

Work 41 rows st st.
Row 51: K1, k2tog, k4, k2tog, k1. (8 sts)
Work 5 rows st st.
Row 57: K1, k2tog, k2, k2tog, k1. (6 sts)
Work 11 rows st st.
Row 69: K1, inc, k2, inc, k1. (8 sts)
Row 70: P1, inc, p4, inc, p1. (10 sts)
Work 10 rows st st.
Row 81: K1, k2tog, k4, k2tog, k1. (8 sts)
Row 82: P1, p2tog, p2, p2tog, p1. (6 sts)
Cast (bind) off.

Inside of Jaws
With pa, cast on 9 sts.
Row 1: Knit.
Row 2: Purl.
Row 3: K1, inc, k5, inc, k1. (11 sts)
Row 4: Purl.
Work 12 rows st st.
Row 17: K1, k2tog, k5, k2tog, k1. (9 sts)
Row 18: P1, p2tog, p3, p2tog, p1. (7 sts)
Work 4 rows st st.
Row 23: Purl.
Row 24: Purl.
Row 25: K1, inc, k3, inc, k1. (9 sts)
Row 26: Purl.
Row 27: K1, inc, k5, inc, k1. (11 sts)
Work 15 rows st st.
Row 43: K1, k2tog, k5, k2tog, k1. (9 sts)
Row 44: Purl.
Row 45: K1, k2tog, k3, k2tog, k1. (7 sts)
Row 46: Purl.
Cast (bind) off.

To Make Up
SEWING IN ENDS Sew in ends, leaving ends from cast on and cast (bound) off rows for sewing up.
LEGS With WS together, fold each leg in half. Sew up each claw and then main leg on RS.
HEAD AND BODY With WS together, sew along back and around tail to 4cm (1½in) from back of back legs. Bend the armature

wire into a 'U' shape and cut to fit down both back legs, with extra to form a triangle shape for feet. Use pliers to shape the feet. Roll a little stuffing around wire and slip wire into body, one end down each back leg. Cut another length of wire to fit from end of tail, up through body along spine and into head, with a loop for the head. Insert wire into tail and through body.

TUMMY Sew cast on row of tummy to where you finished sewing underside of tail. Sew up one side of tummy, leaving 7cm (2¾in) of chin unattached for jaws, then sew up other side of tummy, leaving an 8cm (3in) gap for stuffing.

INSIDE JAWS With WS facing, sew inside jaws to underside of head and the flap left unattached from tummy.

STUFFING Stuff the body; you will not be able to get stuffing right to the end of the tail or feet, but stuff the rest of the Tyrannosaurus Rex very firmly as it will help him stay upright. Lightly stuff his lower jaw as it needs to hang down, then sew up the gap. Mould body into shape.

FRONT LEGS Cut a pipecleaner to fit each front leg, with one end folded over and 3cm (1¼in) extra to stick into body. Roll in stuffing and sew up front leg around it. Push end of pipecleaner into body, approx 7cm (2¾in) down from chin where body meets tummy section. Sew to body and bend into shape.

TEETH With en, sew sixteen 4-loop French knots around upper jaw where inside and outside join, spacing them approx 5mm (¼in) apart. Sew sixteen 2-loop French knots around lower jaw.

EYES With bl, sew four 3cm (1¼in) horizontal stitches approx 2cm (¾in) up from mouth and 6cm (2½in) from end of nose. Sew yellow or gold beads in centre of eyes.

Triceratops

The Triceratops was related to the rhinoceros, but was about the size of an African elephant. With its huge skull, three horns and frill, it was pretty distinctive. The Triceratops was a herbivore but would charge its enemies if annoyed. It was one of the many dinosaurs that were prey for Tyrannosaurus Rex. There is a three-member Japanese rock band called Toraiseratoppusu, which translates as Triceratops.

Triceratops

The Triceratops does not need any pipecleaners or wire so can be made for small children.

Measurements

Length: 41cm (16¼in)
Height to centre back: 14cm (5½in)

Materials

Pair of 2¾mm (US 2) knitting needles
Double-pointed 2¾mm (US 2) knitting needles (for i-cord and for holding stitches)
25g (1oz) of Rowan Felted Tweed in Celadon 184 (ce)
5g (⅙oz) of Rowan Fine Lace in Stoneware 943 (st) used DOUBLE throughout
5g (⅙oz) of Rowan Felted Tweed in Frozen 185 (fr)
Tiny amount of Rowan Pure Wool DK in Black 004 (bl) for eyes
2 tiny black beads for eyes and sewing needle and black thread for sewing on

Abbreviations

See page 78.
See page 79 for I-cord Technique.

Right Back Leg

With ce, cast on 16 sts.
Work 2 rows k1, p1 rib.
Row 3: K2tog, rib to last 2 sts, k2tog. (14 sts)
Work 2 rows rib.
Row 6: K2tog, k10, k2tog. (12 sts)
Work 3 rows st st.
Row 10: K1, inc, k8, inc, k1. (14 sts)
Work 3 rows st st.
Row 14: K1, inc, k10, inc, k1. (16 sts)
Work 3 rows st st.
Row 18: K1, inc, k12, inc, k1. (18 sts)
Row 19: Purl.
Row 20: K1, inc, k14, inc, k1. (20 sts)
Row 21: Purl.
Row 22: K1, inc, k16, inc, k1. (22 sts)
Row 23: Purl.
Row 24: K1, inc, k18, inc, k1. (24 sts)
Row 25: Purl.
Row 26: K1, inc, k20, inc, k1. (26 sts)
Work 7 rows st st.*
Row 34: Cast (bind) off 13 sts, k to end (hold 13 sts on spare needle for Right Side of Body).

Left Back Leg

Work as for Right Back Leg to *.
Row 34: K13, cast (bind) off 13 sts (hold 13 sts on spare needle for Left Side of Body).

Right Front Leg

With ce, cast on 16 sts.
Work 2 rows k1, p1 rib.
Row 3: K2tog, rib to last 2 sts, k2tog. (14 sts)
Work 2 rows rib.
Row 6: K2tog, k10, k2tog. (12 sts)
Work 5 rows st st.
Row 12: K1, inc, k8, inc, k1. (14 sts)
Work 3 rows st st.
Row 16: K1, inc, k10, inc, k1. (16 sts)
Work 3 rows st st.
Row 20: K1, inc, k12, inc, k1. (18 sts)
Work 3 rows st st.
Row 24: K1, inc, k14, inc, k1. (20 sts)

Work 5 rows st st.**
Row 30: Cast (bind) off 10 sts, k to end (hold 10 sts on spare needle for Right Side of Body).

Left Front Leg

Work as for Right Front Leg to **.
Row 30: K10, cast (bind) off 10 sts (hold 10 sts on spare needle for Left Side of Body).

Right Side of Body

With ce, cast on 8 sts.
Row 1: K8, cast on 3 sts. (11 sts)
Row 2: P11, cast on 3 sts. (14 sts)
Row 3: K14, with RS facing k13 from spare needle of Right Back Leg. (27 sts)
Row 4: P12, k2, p13, with WS facing p10 from spare needle of Right Front Leg. (37 sts)
Row 5: K9, p2, k11, p2, k13, cast on 45 sts. (82 sts)
Row 6: Cast (bind) off 10 sts, p48 icos, k2, p11, k2, p9, cast on 5 sts. (77 sts)
Row 7: K15, p2, k10, p2, k48.
Row 8: Cast (bind) off 8 sts, p40 icos, k2, p10, k2, p15, cast on 5 sts. (74 sts)
Row 9: K21, p2, k9, p2, k40.
Row 10: Cast (bind) off 6 sts, p34 icos, k2, p9, k2, p21. (68 sts)
Row 11: K21, p2, k9, p2, k34.
Row 12: Cast (bind) off 4 sts, p30 icos, k2, p9, k2, p21. (64 sts)
Row 13: K21, p2, k10, p2, k29.
Row 14: Cast (bind) off 4 sts, p25 icos, k2, p10, k2, p21. (60 sts)
Row 15: K21, p2, k10, p2, k25.
Row 16: Cast (bind) off 4 sts, p21 icos, k2, p11, k2, p20. (56 sts)
Row 17: K20, p1, k14, p1, k20.
Row 18: Cast (bind) off 4 sts, p16 icos, k1, p14, k1, p20. (52 sts)
Row 19: Knit.
Row 20: Cast (bind) off 4 sts, p to end. (48 sts)

Row 21: Cast (bind) off 8 sts, k to end. (40 sts)
Row 22: P2tog, p to end. (39 sts)
Row 23: Cast (bind) off 3 sts, k34 icos, k2tog. (35 sts)
Row 24: P2tog, p31, p2tog. (33 sts)
Row 25: Cast (bind) off 3 sts, k28 icos, k2tog. (29 sts)
Row 26: P2tog, p25, p2tog. (27 sts)
Row 27: Cast (bind) off 5 sts, k20 icos, k2tog. (21 sts)
Row 28: P2tog, p17, p2tog. (19 sts)
Row 29: Cast (bind) off 6 sts, k to end. (13 sts)
Cast (bind) off.

Left Side of Body
With ce, cast on 8 sts.
Row 1: P8, cast on 3 sts. (11 sts)
Row 2: K11, cast on 3 sts. (14 sts)
Row 3: P14, with WS facing p13 from spare needle of Left Back Leg. (27 sts)
Row 4: K12, p2, k13, with RS facing k10 from spare needle of Left Front Leg. (37 sts)
Row 5: P9, k2, p11, k2, p13, cast on 45 sts. (82 sts)
Row 6 : Cast (bind) off 10 sts, k48 icos, p2, k11, p2, k9, cast on 5 sts. (77 sts)
Row 7: P15, k2, p10, k2, p48.
Row 8: Cast (bind) off 8 sts, k40 icos, p2, k10, p2, k15, cast on 5 sts. (74 sts)
Row 9: P21, k2, p9, k2, p40.
Row 10: Cast (bind) off 6 sts, k34 icos, p2, k9, p2, k21. (68 sts)
Row 11: P21, k2, p9, k2, p34.
Row 12: Cast (bind) off 4 sts, k30 icos, p2, k9, p2, k21. (64 sts)
Row 13: P21, k2, p10, k2, p29.
Row 14: Cast (bind) off 4 sts, k25 icos, p2, k10, p2, k21. (60 sts)
Row 15: P21, k2, p10, k2, p25.
Row 16: Cast (bind) off 4 sts, k21 icos, p2, k11, p2, k20. (56 sts)
Row 17: P20, k1, p14, k1, p20.

Row 18: Cast (bind) off 4 sts, k16 icos, p1, k14, p1, k20. (52 sts)
Row 19: Purl.
Row 20: Cast (bind) off 4 sts, k to end. (48 sts)
Row 21: Cast (bind) off 8 sts, p to end. (40 sts)
Row 22: K2tog, k to end. (39 sts)
Row 23: Cast (bind) off 3 sts, p34 icos, p2tog. (35 sts)
Row 24: K2tog, k31, k2tog. (33 sts)
Row 25: Cast (bind) off 3 sts, p28 icos, p2tog. (29 sts)
Row 26: K2tog, k25, k2tog. (27 sts)
Row 27: Cast (bind) off 5 sts, p20 icos, p2tog. (21 sts)
Row 28: K2tog, k17, k2tog. (19 sts)
Row 29: Cast (bind) off 6 sts, p to end. (13 sts)
Cast (bind) off.

Head
With ce, cast on 1 st.
Row 1: Knit.
Row 2: Inc. (2 sts)
Row 3: Purl.
Row 4: Inc, k1. (3 sts)
Row 5: Purl.
Row 6: Inc, k1, inc. (5 sts)
Row 7: Purl.
Row 8: K1, inc, k1, inc, k1. (7 sts)
Row 9: Purl.
Row 10: K1, inc, k3, inc, k1. (9 sts)
Row 11: Purl.
Join in st.
Row 12: K3ce, incst, k1st, incst, turn.
With double-pointed needles and st, work i-cord on these 5 sts only as folls:
Knit 3 rows.
Next row: K2tog, k1, k2tog. (3 sts)
Next row: Knit.
Next row: K2tog, k1. (2 sts)
Next row: Knit.
Next row: K2tog and fasten off.

With ce, cast on 3 sts, k3. (9 sts)
Row 13: Purl.
Row 14: K1, inc, k5, inc, k1. (11 sts)
Row 15: Purl.
Row 16: K1, inc, k7, inc, k1. (13 sts)
Row 17: Purl.
Row 18: K1, inc, k9, inc, k1. (15 sts)
Row 19: Purl.
Row 20: K1, inc, k11, inc, k1. (17 sts)
Row 21: Purl.
Work 4 rows st st.
Row 26: K1, inc, k13, inc, k1. (19 sts)
Row 27: Purl.
Row 28: K1, inc, k15, inc, k1. (21 sts)
Row 29: Purl.
Join in st.
Row 30: K5ce, *incst, k1st, incst, turn.
With double-pointed needles and st, work
i-cord on these 5 sts only as folls:
Knit 8 rows.
Next row: K2tog, k3. (4 sts)
Knit 4 rows.
Next row: K2tog, k2. (3 sts)
Knit 4 rows.
Next row: K2tog, k1. (2 sts)
Knit 3 rows.
Next row: K2tog and fasten off.
With ce, cast on 3 sts, k5*; rep from * to *
once more.
Row 31: Purl.
Cont in fr.
Work 1 row k1, p1 rib.
Row 33: Inc, [k1, p1, inc, p1, k1, inc] to last
2 sts, k1, inc. (29 sts)
Work 3 rows rib.
Row 37: Inc, rib to last st, inc. (31 sts)
Row 38: Rep row 37. (33 sts)
Row 39: Cast (bind) off 4 sts, rib to end.
(29 sts)
Row 40: Rep row 39. (25 sts)
Row 41: [Rib 1, inc, rib 1] 4 times, rib 1,
[rib 1, inc, rib 1] 4 times. (33 sts)
Work 4 rows rib.
Row 46: [Inc, rib 1] to last st, inc. (50 sts)

Work 1 row rib.
Row 48: Cast (bind) off 5 sts, rib to end.
(45 sts)
Row 49: Rep row 48. (40 sts)
Work 1 row rib.
Change to ce.
Work 1 row rib.
Cast (bind) off.

Tummy
With ce, cast on 1 st.
Row 1: [Inc] twice. (2 sts)
Row 2: Purl.
Work 2 rows st st.
Row 5: [Inc] twice. (4 sts)
Work 3 rows st st.
Row 9: K1, [inc] twice, k1. (6 sts)

Head
The Triceratops has a ribbed frill
and three horns, which are all
knitted in as part of the head.

Row 10: P2, inc, p3. (7 sts)
Row 11: K3, p1, k3.
Row 12: P1, inc, p1, k1, p1, inc, p1. (9 sts)
Row 13: K4, p1, k4.
Row 14: P4, k1, p4.
Rep rows 13–14, 22 times more.
Work 6 rows st st.
Row 65: K2tog, k5, k2tog. (7 sts)

Work 7 rows st st.

Work 2 rows moss (seed) st.

Row 75: K2tog, moss (seed) st 3, k2tog. (5 sts)

Work 12 rows moss (seed) st.

Row 88: K2tog, p1, k2tog. (3 sts)

Work 5 rows moss (seed) st.

Row 94: K3tog and fasten off.

To Make up

SEWING IN ENDS Sew in ends, leaving ends from cast on and cast (bound) off rows for sewing up.

LEGS With WS together, fold each leg in half and sew up on RS, starting at feet.

BODY AND TAIL With WS together, sew along back and down tail to approx 2cm (¾in) behind back legs.

HEAD Sew head onto body where the two sides of body meet for the neck (where ce meets fr), with nose pointing forwards.

TUMMY With RS of body and WS of tummy (reverse st st side) together, sew cast on row of tummy to top of tail, and sew cast (bound) off row to end of nose. Ease and sew tummy to fit body, leaving a 2.5cm (1in) gap between front and back legs on one side.

STUFFING Stuff the Triceratops very firmly to make him stand up (the horns do not need any stuffing). Sew up the gap and mould the body into shape.

NOSE Sew tip of nose down to chin approx 5mm (¼in) as in photograph.

TOENAILS With st, sew four toenails around the front of each foot, using 3 horizontal satin stitches per toenail.

EYES With bl, sew 2-loop French knots positioned as in photograph, 3 sts in front of horns with 6 sts between eyes. Sew black beads on top of knots.

Archelon

The largest sea turtle ever known, weighing more than 4,000 pounds, the Archelon lived in North America, which was then mainly covered by sea. A slow mover, the Archelon swam near the surface of the sea and lived for up to 100 years, possibly thanks to taking long sleeps on the seabed, and only ventured onto land to lay eggs.

Archelon

The Archelon's shell is sewn on after knitting the whole body.

Measurements

Length: 19cm (7½in)
Height to top of shell: 7cm (2¾in)

Materials

Pair of 3¼mm (US 3) knitting needles
35g (1⅜oz) of Rowan Alpaca Colour in Agate 137 (ag)
15g (½oz) of Rowan Alpaca Colour in Iron 135 (ir)
Tiny amount of Rowan Pure Wool 4ply in Black 404 (bl) for eyes

Abbreviations

See page 78.

Back Flippers

(make 2 the same)
With ag, cast on 4 sts.
Beg with a k row, work 2 rows st st.
Row 3: K1, [inc] twice, k1. (6 sts)
Row 4: Purl.
Row 5: K2, [inc] twice, k2. (8 sts)
Row 6: Purl.
Row 7: Inc, k2, [inc] twice, k2, inc. (12 sts)
Row 8: Purl.
Row 9: Inc, k10, inc. (14 sts)
Work 3 rows st st.
Row 13: K2tog, k10, k2tog. (12 sts)
Row 14: Purl.
Cast (bind) off.

Front Flippers

(make 2 the same)
With ag, cast on 2 sts.
Beg with a k row, work 2 rows st st.
Row 3: [Inc] twice. (4 sts)
Row 4: Purl.
Row 5: K1, [inc] twice, k1. (6 sts)
Row 6: Purl.
Row 7: K2, [inc] twice, k2. (8 sts)
Row 8: Purl.
Row 9: Inc, k2, [inc] twice, k2, inc. (12 sts)
Row 10: Purl.
Row 11: Inc, k10, inc. (14 sts)
Row 12: Purl.
Row 13: K3, inc, k6, inc, k3. (16 sts)
Work 3 rows st st.
Row 17: K4, inc, k6, inc, k4. (18 sts)
Work 5 rows st st.
Row 23: K2tog, k14, k2tog. (16 sts)
Row 24: Purl.
Row 25: K2tog, k12, k2tog. (14 sts)
Row 26: Purl.
Row 27: K2tog, k10, k2tog. (12 sts)
Work 3 rows st st.
Cast (bind) off.

Underside of Body and Head

With ag, cast on 2 sts.
Beg with a k row, work 2 rows st st.
Row 3: [Inc] twice. (4 sts)
Work 5 rows st st.
Row 9: K4, cast on 6 sts. (10 sts)
Row 10: P10, cast on 6 sts. (16 sts)
Row 11: K16, cast on 3 sts. (19 sts)
Row 12: P19, cast on 3 sts. (22 sts)
Row 13: Knit.
Row 14: Purl.
Row 15: Inc, k20, inc. (24 sts)
Work 3 rows st st.
Row 19: Inc, k22, inc. (26 sts)
Work 29 rows st st.
Row 49: K2tog, k22, k2tog. (24 sts)
Work 9 rows st st.
Row 59: K2tog, k20, k2tog. (22 sts)
Row 60: Purl.
Row 61: Cast (bind) off 4 sts, k to end. (18 sts)
Row 62: Cast (bind) off 4 sts, p to end. (14 sts)
Row 63: Cast (bind) off 4 sts, k to end. (10 sts)
Row 64: Cast (bind) off 4 sts, p to end. (6 sts)
Work 8 rows st st.
Row 73: K1, [k2tog] twice, k1. (4 sts)
Row 74: Purl.
Row 75: [K2tog] twice. (2 sts)
Row 76: P2tog and fasten off.

Top of Body and Head

With ag, cast on 2 sts.
Beg with a k row, work 2 rows st st.
Row 3: [Inc] twice. (4 sts)
Work 5 rows st st.
Row 9: K4, cast on 6 sts. (10 sts)
Row 10: P10, cast on 6 sts. (16 sts)
Row 11: K16, cast on 3 sts. (19 sts)
Row 12: P19, cast on 3 sts. (22 sts)
Row 13: Knit.
Row 14: Purl.
Row 15: Inc, k3, [inc] twice, k4, [inc] twice,

Nose

Pull the top of the nose over the bottom to create a point.

k4, [inc] twice, k3, inc. (30 sts)
Work 3 rows st st.
Row 19: Inc, k13, [inc] twice, k13, inc.
(34 sts)
Work 3 rows st st.
Row 23: K9, inc, k6, [inc] twice, k6, inc, k9.
(38 sts)
Work 3 rows st st.
Row 27: K18, [inc] twice, k18. (40 sts)
Work 3 rows st st.
Row 31: K10, inc, k8, [inc] twice, k8, inc,
k10. (44 sts)
Work 5 rows st st.
Row 37: K10, k2tog, k8, [k2tog] twice, k8,
k2tog, k10. (40 sts)
Work 3 rows st st.
Row 41: K2tog, k6, [k2tog] twice, k6, [k2tog]
twice, k6, [k2tog] twice, k6, k2tog. (32 sts)
Work 3 rows st st.
Row 45: K6, k2tog, k6, [k2tog] twice, k6,
k2tog, k6. (28 sts)
Work 3 rows st st.
Row 49: K2tog, k24, k2tog. (26 sts)
Row 50: Purl.
Row 51: K2tog, k9, [k2tog] twice, k9, k2tog.
(22 sts)
Row 52: Purl.
Row 53: Cast (bind) off 4 sts, k to end.
(18 sts)
Row 54: Cast (bind) off 4 sts, p to end.
(14 sts)
Row 55: Cast (bind) off 4 sts, k to end.
(10 sts)
Row 56: Cast (bind off) 4 sts, p to end. (6 sts)
Row 57: K1, [inc] 4 times, k1. (10 sts)
Row 58: P1, inc, p2, [inc] twice, p2, inc, p1.
(14 sts)

Work 6 rows st st.
Row 65: K1, [k2tog] twice, k4, [k2tog] twice,
k1. (10 sts)
Row 66: P2, p2tog, p2, p2tog, p2. (8 sts)
Row 67: K1, [k2tog] 3 times, k1. (5 sts)
Row 68: P2tog, p1, p2tog. (3 sts)
Row 69: K3tog and fasten off.

Shell

With ir, cast on 21 sts.
Row 1: Moss (seed) st 8, k2, p1, k2, moss
(seed) st 8.
Row 2: Moss (seed) st 8, p2, k1, p2, moss
(seed) st 8, cast on 2 sts. (23 sts)
Row 3: Moss (seed) st 10, k2, p1, k2, moss
(seed) st 8, cast on 2 sts. (25 sts)
Row 4: Inc, moss (seed) st 9, p1, inc, k1, inc,
p1, moss (seed) st 9, inc. (29 sts)
Row 5: Moss (seed) st 12, k2, p1, k2, moss
(seed) st 12.
Row 6: Moss (seed) st 12, p2, k1, p2, moss
(seed) st 12.
Row 7: Inc, moss (seed) st 11, k2, p1, k2,
moss (seed) st 11, inc. (31 sts)
Row 8: Moss (seed) st 13, p2, k1, p2, moss
(seed) st 13.
Row 9: Inc, moss (seed) st 5, [inc] twice,
moss (seed) st 5, k2, p1, k2, moss (seed) st 5,
[inc] twice, moss (seed) st 5, inc. (37 sts)
Row 10: Moss (seed) st 16, p2, k1, p2, moss
(seed) st 16.
Row 11: Moss (seed) st 16, k2, p1, k2, moss
(seed) st 16.
Row 12: Moss (seed) st 16, p1, inc, k1, inc,
p1, moss (seed) st 16. (39 sts)
Row 13: Moss (seed) st 17, k2, p1, k2, moss
(seed) st 17.

Row 14: Moss (seed) st 17, p2, k1, p2, moss (seed) st 17.

Row 15: Moss (seed) st 17, k2, p1, k2, moss (seed) st 17.

Rep rows 14–15 once more.

Row 18: Inc, moss (seed) st 16, p2, k1, p2, moss (seed) st 16, inc. (41 sts)

Row 19: Moss (seed) st 18, k2, p1, k2, moss (seed) st 18.

Row 20: Moss (seed) st 18, p2, k1, p2, moss (seed) st 18.

Rep rows 19–20 twice more.

Row 25: Moss (seed) st 18, k1, inc, p1, inc, k1, moss (seed) st 18. (43 sts)

Row 26: Moss (seed) st 19, p2, k1, p2, moss (seed) st 19.

Row 27: Moss (seed) st 19, k2, p1, k2, moss (seed) st 19.

Rep rows 26–27, 4 times more.

Row 36: Moss (seed) st 18, p1, p2tog, k1, p2tog, p1, moss (seed) st 18. (41 sts)

Row 37: Moss (seed) st 18, k2, p1, k2, moss (seed) st 18.

Row 38: Moss (seed) st 18, p2, k1, p2, moss (seed) st 18.

Rep rows 37–38 twice more.

Row 43: P2tog, moss (seed) st 16, k2, p1, k2, moss (seed) st 16, p2tog. (39 sts)

Row 44: Moss (seed) st 17, p2, k1, p2, moss (seed) st 17.

Row 45: Moss (seed) st 17, k2, p1, k2, moss (seed) st 17.

Rep rows 44–45 once more.

Row 48: K2tog, moss (seed) st 14, p1, p2tog, k1, p2tog, p1, moss (seed) st 14, k2tog. (35 sts)

Row 49: Moss (seed) st 15, k2, p1, k2, moss (seed) st 15.

Row 50: Moss (seed) st 6, k2tog, p2tog, moss (seed) st 5, p2, k1, p2, moss (seed) st 5, p2tog, k2tog, moss (seed) st 6. (31 sts)

Row 51: Moss (seed) st 13, k2, p1, k2, moss (seed) st 13.

Row 52: P2tog, moss (seed) st 10, p1, p2tog, k1, p2tog, p1, moss (seed) st 10, p2tog. (27 sts)

Row 53: Moss (seed) st 11, k2, p1, k2, moss (seed) st 11.

Row 54: K2tog, moss (seed) st 9, p2, k1, p2, moss (seed) st 9, k2tog. (25 sts)

Row 55: Cast (bind) off 4 sts, moss (seed) st 6 icos, k2, p1, k2, moss (seed) st 10. (21 sts)

Row 56: Cast (bind) off 4 sts, moss (seed) st 6 icos, p2, k1, p2, moss (seed) st 6. (17 sts)
Cast (bind) off.

To Make Up

SEWING IN ENDS Sew in ends, leaving ends from cast on and cast (bound) off rows for sewing up.

FLIPPERS With WS together, fold each flipper in half and sew up on RS, starting at cast on edge. Stuff each flipper and sew along top, leaving an end to use for attaching to body.

BODY AND HEAD With WS together, sew around tail, body and head (make sure the nose is pointy), leaving a 2.5cm (1in) gap on one side.

STUFFING Starting at head, stuff the Archelon firmly, then sew up the gap. Mould body into shape.

ATTACHING FLIPPERS Sew the front flippers to the seam on the body, positioned 3 sts from neck. Attach the back flippers, starting 6 sts from tail.

SHELL Attach the shell to top of body, using running stitch and sewing one stitch in from the edge. The stitches can be quite big and not too tight to give the feel of the shell sitting on top of the body.

EYES With bl, sew 2-loop French knots positioned as in photograph.

Pterodactyl

Not strictly speaking a dinosaur at all, the Pterodactyl or 'winged finger' is an extinct flying carnivorous reptile. In the original 1933 film *King Kong*, Kong battled with and finally defeated an enormous Pterodactyl that tried to steal Fay Wray. Chicago-based heavy metal band Pterodactyl King claim to have been 'forged in the depths of an active volcano 6,000 years ago'.

Pterodactyl

The Pterodactyl is fairly simple to knit.

Measurements
Height: 17cm (6¾in)
Wingspan: 36cm (14in)

Materials
Pair of 2¾mm (US 2) knitting needles
15g (½oz) of Rowan Tweed in Reeth 596 (re)
15g (½oz) of Rowan Fine Lace in Stoneware 943 (st)
Tiny amount of Rowan Pure Wool 4ply in Black 404 (bl) for eyes
2 tiny black beads for eyes and sewing needle and black thread for sewing on
2 pipecleaners for wings and 1 pipecleaner for legs, neck and head

Abbreviations
See page 78.
See page 79 for Wrap and Turn Method.

Right Leg
With re, cast on 4 sts.
Beg with a k row, work 8 rows st st.
Row 9: K1, [inc] twice, k1. (6 sts)
Work 5 rows st st.*
Row 15: K3, cast (bind) off 3 sts (hold 3 sts on spare needle for Back and Head).

Left Leg
Work as for Right Back Leg to *.
Row 15: Cast (bind) off 3 sts, k to end (hold 3 sts on spare needle for Back and Head).

Back and Head
Row 1: With re and RS facing, k3 from

spare needle of Right Leg, cast on 4 sts, then k3 from spare needle of Left Leg. (10 sts)
Row 2: Purl.
Work 10 rows st st.
Row 13: K1, inc. k6, inc, k1. (12 sts)
Work 11 rows st st.
Row 25: K2tog, k8, k2tog. (10 sts)
Row 26: Purl.
Row 27: K10, cast on 40 sts. (50 sts)
Row 28: Purl.
Work 3 rows st st.
Row 32: Cast (bind) off 40 sts, p to end. (10 sts)
Row 33: Knit.
Row 34: Cast (bind) off 3 sts, p to end. (7 sts)
Row 35: Cast (bind) off 3 sts, k to end. (4 sts)
Work 3 rows st st.
Row 39: K4, cast on 5 sts. (9 sts)
Row 40: P9, cast on 3 sts, (12 sts)
Row 41: K12, cast on 6 sts. (18 sts)
Row 42: P18, cast on 4 sts (22 sts)
Row 43: Cast (bind) off 3 sts, k17 icos, k2tog. (18 sts)
Row 44: Cast (bind) off 3 sts, p13 icos, p2tog. (14 sts)
Row 45: Cast (bind) off 3 sts, k9 icos, k2tog. (10 sts)
Row 46: Cast (bind) off 6 sts, p to end. (4 sts)
Cast (bind) off.

Front and Head
With re, cast on 10 sts.
Row 1: Knit.
Work 10 rows st st.
Row 12: P1, inc, p6, inc, p1. (12 sts)
Work 11 rows st st.
Row 24: P2tog, p8, p2tog. (10 sts)
Row 25: K10, cast on 40 sts. (50 sts)
Work 4 rows st st.
Row 30: Cast (bind) off 40 sts, p to end. (10 sts)
Row 31: Knit.
Row 32: Cast (bind) off 3 sts, p to end. (7 sts)
Row 33: Cast (bind) off 3 sts, k to end. (4 sts)
Work 4 rows st st.

Row 38: P4, cast on 5 sts. (9 sts)
Row 39: K9, cast on 3 sts. (12 sts)
Row 40: P12, cast on 6 sts. (18 sts)
Row 41: K18, cast on 4 sts. (22 sts)
Row 42: Cast (bind) off 3 sts, p17 icos, p2tog. (18 sts)
Row 43: Cast (bind) off 3 sts, k13 icos, k2tog. (14 sts)
Row 44: Cast (bind) off 3 sts, p9 icos, p2tog. (10 sts)
Row 45: Cast (bind) off 6 sts, k to end. (4 sts)
Cast (bind) off.

Wings
(make 2 the same)
With st, cast on 2 sts.
Beg with a k row, work 2 rows st st.
Row 3: [Inc] twice. (4 sts)
Row 4: Purl.
Work 2 rows st st.
Row 7: K1, [inc] twice, k1. (6 sts)
Work 3 rows st st.
Row 11: K1, inc, k2, inc, k1. (8 sts)
Work 3 rows st st.
Row 15: K1, inc, k4, inc, k1. (10 sts)
Work 3 rows st st.
Row 19: K1, inc, k6, inc, k1. (12 sts)
Work 3 rows st st.
Row 23: K1, inc, k8, inc, k1. (14 sts)
Work 5 rows st st.
Row 29: K1, inc, k10, inc, k1. (16 sts)
Work 5 rows st st.
Row 35: K1, inc, k12, inc, k1. (18 sts)
Work 5 rows st st.
Row 41: K1, inc, k14, inc, k1. (20 sts)
Work 7 rows st st.
Row 49: K1, inc, k16, inc, k1. (22 sts)
Work 11 rows st st.
Row 61: K1, k2tog, k16, k2tog, k1. (20 sts)
Work 7 rows st st.
Row 69: K1, k2tog, k14, k2tog, k1. (18 sts)
Work 5 rows st st.
Row 75: K1, k2tog, k12, k2tog, k1. (16 sts)
Work 3 rows st st.

Row 79: K1, k2tog, k10, k2tog, k1. (14 sts)
Work 3 rows st st.
Row 83: K1, k2tog, k8, k2tog, k1. (12 sts)
Work 3 rows st st.
Row 87: K1, k2tog, k6, k2tog, k1. (10 sts)
Work 3 rows st st.
Row 91: K1, k2tog, k4, k2tog, k1. (8 sts)
Row 92: Purl.
Row 93: K1, k2tog, k2, k2tog, k1. (6 sts)
Row 94: Purl.
Row 95: K1, [k2tog] twice, k1. (4 sts)
Row 96: Purl.
Row 97: [K2tog] twice. (2 sts)
Row 98: Purl.
Row 99: K2tog and fasten off.

To Make Up
SEWING IN ENDS Sew in ends, leaving ends
from cast on row and cast (bound) off rows
for sewing up.
LEGS AND BODY With WS together, sew up
legs and across bottom. Fold a pipecleaner
into a 'U' shape and slip one end down
each leg, with 1cm (½in) sticking out of feet.
Wrap end of pipecleaner with st and make
two 1cm (½in) loops in st either side of
pipecleaner to indicate claws.
HEAD Sew two sides of head together. Slip a
pipecleaner into head and 4cm (1½in) down
body, with ends folded over to stop it from
poking out.
BODY Sew up sides of body, leaving a 2.5cm
(1in) gap. Stuff firmly and sew up gap.
ARMS AND WINGS Cut a pipecleaner to fit
each arm, with one end folded over. Sew up
arm around pipecleaner. Press wings and
then sew to arm seams and down length of
body to end of knitted leg.
EYES With bl, sew 3-loop French knots,
1 st down from top of head and approx 8 sts
from back point of head. Sew black beads on
top of knots.
CLAWS With st, make 3 loops on each arm,
6cm (2½in) from where arm meets body.

Wings
**The wings can be sewn either way,
as the Pterodactyl is the same on
both sides.**

Stegosaurus

The Stegosaurus is one of the most recognisable dinosaurs, due to the distinctive plates running along its spine. About the size of a bus, the Stegosaurus was a gentle herbivore and often considered to be a little unsophisticated due to its small brain, no larger than a dog's. Because a fossil was found there, the Stegosaurus is the state dinosaur of Colorado. The Stegosaurus has featured in many films, including *King Kong*, and is an integral part of the plot in *The Lost World* by Arthur Conan Doyle.

Stegosaurus

An impressive and simple dinosaur to knit, the Stegosaurus needs lots of stuffing.

Measurements
Length: 33cm (13in)
Height to centre back (including plates): 25cm (10in)

Materials
Pair of 3¼mm (US 3) knitting needles
Double-pointed 3¼mm (US 3) knitting needles (for holding stitches)
45g (1¾oz) of Rowan Tweed in Bedale 581 (be)
10g (¼oz) of Rowan Felted Tweed in Celadon 184 (ce)
10g (¼oz) of Rowan Felted Tweed in Ginger 154 (gn)
2 tiny black beads for eyes and sewing needle and black thread for sewing on
2 pipecleaners for legs

Abbreviations
See page 78.

Right Back Leg
With be, cast on 15 sts.
Beg with a k row, work 2 rows st st.
Row 3: Inc, k4, k2tog, k1, k2tog, k4, inc. (15 sts)
Row 4: P5, p2tog, p1, p2tog, p5. (13 sts)
Row 5: K4, k2tog, k1, k2tog, k4. (11 sts)
Work 5 rows st st.
Row 11: Inc, k9, inc. (13 sts)
Work 3 rows st st.

Row 15: Inc, k11, inc. (15 sts)
Work 3 rows st st.
Row 19: K6, inc, k1, inc, k6. (17 sts)
Work 5 rows st st.*
Row 25: Cast (bind) off 8 sts, k to end (hold 9 sts on spare needle for Right Side of Body and Head).

Left Back Leg
Work as for Right Back Leg to *.
Row 25: K9, cast (bind) off 8 sts (hold 9 sts on spare needle for Left Side of Body and Head).

Right Front Leg
With be, cast on 13 sts.
Beg with a k row, work 2 rows st st.
Row 3: Inc, k3, k2tog, k1, k2tog, k3, inc. (13 sts)
Row 4: P4, p2tog, p1, p2tog, p4. (11 sts)
Row 5: K3, k2tog, k1, k2tog, k3. (9 sts)
Work 5 rows st st.
Row 11: Inc, k7, inc. (11 sts)
Work 3 rows st st.
Row 15: Inc, k9, inc. (13 sts)
Work 5 rows st st.**
Row 21: Cast (bind) off 6 sts, k to end (hold 7 sts on spare needle for Right Side of Body).

Left Front Leg
Work as for Right Front Leg to **.
Row 21: K7, cast (bind) off 6 sts (hold 7 sts on spare needle for Left Side of Body and Head).

Right Side of Body and Head
Row 1: With be, cast on 1 st, with RS facing k7 from spare needle of Right Front Leg, cast on 8 sts. (16 sts)
Row 2: Purl.
Row 3: Inc, k15, cast on 5 sts, with RS facing p1, k3, inc, k4 from spare needle of Right Back Leg, cast on 1 st. (33 sts)
Row 4: P11, k1, p21.

Row 5: Inc, k20, p1, k4, inc, k4, p1, inc. (36 sts)
Row 6: P2, k1, p10, k1, p22, cast on 8 sts. (44 sts)
Row 7: K30, p1, k5, inc, k4, p1, k2, cast on 24 sts. (69 sts)
Row 8: Cast (bind) off 2 sts, p24 icos, k1, p11, k1, p30, cast on 4 sts. (71 sts)
Row 9: K34, p1, k12, p1, k23.
Row 10: Cast (bind) off 3 sts, p20 icos, k1, p12, k1, p34. (68 sts)
Row 11: K34, p1, k12, p1, k20.
Row 12: Cast (bind) off 2 sts, p17 icos, k1, p13, k1, p27, cast (bind) off 2 sts, p to end. (59 sts and 5 sts)
Row 13: Working on 5 sts for head only, k2tog, k3. (4 sts)
Cast (bind) off.
Row 13: Rejoin be to rem 59 sts, k28, p1, k12, p1, k15, k2tog. (58 sts)
Row 14: P2tog, p14, k1, p12, k1, p26, p2tog. (56 sts)
Row 15: K2tog, k25, p1, k13, p1, k12, k2tog. (54 sts)
Row 16: P2tog, p11, k1, p13, k1, p24, p2tog. (52 sts)
Row 17: K2tog, k23, p1, k13, p1, k12. (51 sts)
Row 18: P2tog, p9, k1, p14, k1, p22, p2tog. (49 sts)
Row 19: K24, p1, k13, p1, k10.
Row 20: P2tog, p8, k1, p13, k1, p22, p2tog. (47 sts)
Row 21: K23, p1, k13, p1, k9.
Row 22: P2tog, p20, k1, p22, p2tog. (45 sts)
Row 23: K23, p1, k21.
Row 24: P2tog, p18, k1, p22, p2tog. (43 sts)
Row 25: K23, p1, k19.
Row 26: P2tog, p16, k1, p22, p2tog. (41 sts)
Row 27: K2tog, k21, p1, k17. (40 sts)
Row 28: P2tog, p14, k1, p21, p2tog. (38 sts)
Row 29: K2tog, k21, p1, k14. (37 sts)
Row 30: P2tog, p33, p2tog. (35 sts)
Row 31: K2tog, k33. (34 sts)
Row 32: P2tog, p30, p2tog. (32 sts)

Row 33: K2tog, k30. (31 sts)
Row 34: P2tog, p27, p2tog. (29 sts)
Row 35: K2tog, k27. (28 sts)
Row 36: P2tog, p24, p2tog. (26 sts)
Row 37: K2tog, k24. (25 sts)
Row 38: P2tog, p21, p2tog. (23 sts)
Row 39: Cast (bind) off 3 sts, k18 icos, k2tog. (19 sts)
Row 40: Cast (bind) off 2 sts, p to end. (17 sts)
Row 41: Cast (bind) off 3 sts, k to end. (14 sts)
Row 42: Cast (bind) off 3 sts, p to end. (11 sts)
Cast (bind) off.

Left Side of Body and Head
Row 1: With be, cast on 1 st, with WS facing p7 from spare needle of Left Front Leg, cast on 8 sts. (16 sts)
Row 2: Knit.
Row 3: Inc, p15, cast on 5 sts, with WS facing k1, p3, inc, p4 from spare needle of Left Back Leg, cast on 1 st. (33 sts)
Row 4: K11, p1, k21.
Row 5: Inc, p20, k1, p4, inc, p4, k1, inc. (36 sts)
Row 6: K2, p1, k10, p1, k22, cast on 8 sts. (44 sts)
Row 7: P30, k1, p5, inc, p4, k1, p2, cast on 24 sts. (69 sts)
Row 8: Cast (bind) off 2 sts, k24 icos, p1, k11, p1, k30, cast on 4 sts. (71 sts)
Row 9: P34, k1, p12, k1, p23.
Row 10: Cast (bind) off 3 sts, k20 icos, p1, k12, p1, k34. (68 sts)
Row 11: P34, k1, p12, k1, p20.
Row 12: Cast (bind) off 2 sts, k17 icos, p1, k13, p1, k27, cast (bind) off 2 sts, k to end. (59 sts and 5 sts)
Row 13: Working on 5 sts for head only, p3, p2tog. (4 sts)
Cast (bind) off.
Row 13: Rejoin be to rem 59 sts, p28, k1,

p12, k1, p15, p2tog. (58 sts)
Row 14: K2tog, k14, p1, k12, p1, k26, k2tog. (56 sts)
Row 15: P2tog, p25, k1, p13, k1, p12, p2tog. (54 sts)
Row 16: K2tog, k11, p1, k13, p1, k24, k2tog. (52 sts)
Row 17: P2tog, p23, k1, p13, k1, p12. (51 sts)
Row 18: K2tog, k9, p1, k14, p1, k22, k2tog. (49 sts)
Row 19: P24, k1, p13, k1, p10.
Row 20: K2tog, k8, p1, k13, p1, k22, k2tog. (47 sts)
Row 21: P23, k1, p13, k1, p9.
Row 22: K2tog, k20, p1, k22, k2tog. (45 sts)
Row 23: P23, k1, p21.
Row 24: K2tog, k18, p1, k22, k2tog. (43 sts)
Row 25: P23, k1, p19.
Row 26: K2tog, k16, p1, k22, k2tog. (41 sts)
Row 27: P2tog, p21, k1, p17. (40 sts)
Row 28: K2tog, k14, p1, k21, k2tog. (38 sts)
Row 29: P2tog, p21, k1, p14. (37 sts)
Row 30: K2tog, k33, k2tog. (35 sts)
Row 31: P2tog, p33. (34 sts)
Row 32: K2tog, k30, k2tog. (32 sts)
Row 33: P2tog, p30. (31 sts)
Row 34: K2tog, k27, k2tog. (29 sts)
Row 35: P2tog, p27. (28 sts)
Row 36: K2tog, k24, k2tog. (26 sts)
Row 37: P2tog, p24. (25 sts)
Row 38: K2tog, k21, k2tog. (23 sts)
Row 39: Cast (bind) off 3 sts, p18 icos, p2tog. (19 sts)
Row 40: Cast (bind) off 2 sts, k to end. (17 sts)
Row 41: Cast (bind) off 3 sts, p to end. (14 sts)
Row 42: Cast (bind) off 3 sts, k to end. (11 sts)
Cast (bind) off.

Plates

The plates are sewn along the spine; the quantity is up to you.

Tummy

With be, cast on 2 sts.

Beg with a k row, work 2 rows st st.

Row 3: [Inc] twice. (4 sts)

Work 3 rows st st.

Row 7: Inc, k2, inc. (6 sts)

Work 3 rows st st.

Row 11: Inc, k4, inc. (8 sts)

Work 7 rows st st.

Row 19: Inc, k6, inc. (10 sts)

Work 21 rows st st.

Row 41: K2tog, k6, k2tog. (8 sts)

Row 42: Purl.

Row 43: K2tog, k4, k2tog. (6 sts)

Work 7 rows st st.

Row 51: K2tog, k2, k2tog. (4 sts)

Work 5 rows st st.

Row 57: [K2tog] twice. (2 sts)

Row 58: Purl.

Cast (bind) off.

Large Central Plates

(make 4 in ce and 4 in gn)

With ce/gn, cast on 6 sts.

Knit 2 rows.

Row 3: Inc, k4, inc. (8 sts)

Row 4: Knit.

Row 5: Inc, k6, inc. (10 sts)

Row 6: Knit.

Row 7: K2tog, k6, k2tog. (8 sts)

Knit 2 rows.

Row 10: K2tog, k4, k2tog. (6 sts)

Knit 2 rows.

Row 13: K2tog, k2, k2tog. (4 sts)

Knit 2 rows.

Row 16: [K2tog] twice. (2 sts)

Row 17: Knit.

Row 18: K2tog and fasten off.

Medium Plates

(make 3 in ce and 3 in gn)

With ce/gn, cast on 4 sts.

Knit 2 rows.

Row 3: Inc, k2, inc. (6 sts)

Row 4: Knit.

Row 5: Inc, k4, inc. (8 sts)

Row 6: Knit.

Row 7: K2tog, k4, k2tog. (6 sts)

Knit 2 rows.

Row 10: K2tog, k2, k2tog. (4 sts)

Knit 2 rows.

Row 13: [K2tog] twice. (2 sts)

Row 14: Knit.

Row 15: K2tog and fasten off.

Small Plates

(make 2 in ce and 2 in gn)

With ce/gn, cast on 4 sts.

Knit 2 rows.

Row 3: Inc, k2, inc. (6 sts)

Row 4: Knit.

Row 5: K2tog, k2, k2tog. (4 sts)

Knit 2 rows.

Row 8: [K2tog] twice. (2 sts)

Row 9: Knit.

Row 10: K2tog and fasten off.

Smallest Plates

(make 1 in ce and 1 in gn)

With ce/gn, cast on 2 sts.

Knit 2 rows.

Row 3: [Inc] twice. (4 sts)

Knit 1 row.

Row 5: [K2tog] twice. (2 sts)

Knit 1 row.

Row 7: K2tog and fasten off.

Tail Spikes

(make 4 the same)

With ce, cast on 4 sts.

Beg with a k row, work 10 rows st st.

Cast (bind) off.

To Make Up

SEWING IN ENDS Sew in ends, leaving ends from cast on and cast (bound) off rows for sewing up.

LEGS With WS together, fold each leg in half and sew up on RS, starting at feet.

HEAD AND BODY With WS together and starting at neck, sew around head, along back and around tail to 3cm (1¼in) from back of back legs.

TUMMY Sew cast on row of tummy to back of back legs, and sew cast (bound) off row to front of front legs. Ease and sew tummy to fit body, leaving a 2.5cm (1in) gap between front and back legs on one side.

STUFFING Pipecleaners are used to stiffen the legs and help bend them into shape. Fold a pipecleaner into a 'U' shape and measure against the front two legs. Cut to approximately fit, leaving an extra 2.5cm (1in) at both ends. Fold over the ends. Roll a little stuffing around pipecleaner and slip into the body, one end down each front leg. Repeat with second pipecleaner and back legs. Starting at the head, stuff the Stegosaurus firmly, especially at the thighs, then sew up the gap. Mould body into shape.

PLATES Starting in the centre of the back, sew on the large central plates, alternating the colours and staggering the plates one on one side of the backbone and one on the other side. Sew on the medium plates, two on the left of the central plates and two on the right. Continue as in photograph, with the plates getting smaller towards the head and tail.

TAIL SPIKES With WS together, fold each spike in half and sew up, then attach to tail as in photograph.

EYES Sew on black beads positioned as in photograph.

Velociraptor

A carnivore, the small Velociraptor has strong claws for grabbing prey. A gang of aggressive Velociraptors attack and kill the gamekeeper, Robert Muldoon, in the first *Jurassic Park* film. Toronto named their baseball team the Raptors, and in Australia the garage band Velociraptors consists of 12 raptors.

Velociraptor

Slightly fiddly but worth the effort, the Velociraptor is a rewarding knit.

Measurements
Length: 17cm (6¾in)
Height to top of head: 16cm (6¼in)

Materials
Pair of 2¾mm (US 2) knitting needles
Double-pointed 2¾mm (US 2) knitting needles (for holding stitches)
Small amount of Rowan Pure Wool 4ply in Black 404 (bl) for claws and eyes
15g (½oz) of Rowan Felted Tweed in Avocado 161 (av)
5g (⅛oz) of Rowan Felted Tweed in Treacle 145 (te)
5g (⅛oz) of Rowan Felted Tweed in Stone 190 (st)
Small amount of Rowan Felted Tweed in Rage 150 (ra) for mouth
Small amount of Rowan Pure Wool 4ply in Snow 412 (sn) for teeth
3 pipecleaners for legs and tail

Abbreviations
See page 78.
See page 79 for Colour Knitting.
See page 79 for Wrap and Turn Method.

Right Back Leg
Claws (make 3)
With bl, cast on 1 st.
Row 1: Knit.
Row 2: Inc. (2 sts)

Row 3: [Inc] twice. (4 sts)
Row 4: Purl.
Row 5: Knit.
Row 6: Cast (bind) off 1 st, p1 icos, p2tog (hold 2 sts on spare needle for working leg). Rep from beg twice more. (6 sts on spare needle in total)
Shape leg
Row 7: With av, cast on 2 sts, with RS facing k6 from spare needle of Claws, cast on 2 sts. (10 sts)
Row 8: Purl.
Row 9: K2, k2tog, k2, k2tog, k2. (8 sts)
Row 10: Purl.
Row 11: K1, k2tog, k2, k2tog, k1. (6 sts)
Work 5 rows st st.
Row 17: K2, [inc] twice, k2. (8 sts)
Work 3 rows st st.
Row 21: Inc, k6, inc. (10 sts)
Row 22: Purl.
Row 23: K4, [inc] twice, k4. (12 sts)
Row 24: Purl.
Row 25: Inc, k4, [inc] twice, k4, inc. (16 sts)
Work 3 rows st st.
Row 29: Inc, k6, [inc] twice, k6, inc. (20 sts)
Work 3 rows st st.*
Row 33: Cast (bind) off 10 sts, k to end (hold 10 sts on spare needle for Right Side of Body).

Left Back Leg
Work as for Right Back Leg to *.
Row 33: K10, cast (bind) off 10 sts (hold 10 sts on spare needle for Left Side of Body).

Front Legs
(make 2 the same)
Claws (make 2 for each leg)
With bl, cast on 1 st.
Row 1: Knit.
Row 2: Inc. (2 sts)
Row 3: [Inc] twice. (4 sts)
Row 4: Purl.
Row 5: Knit.

Legs
Once stuffed, bend the legs to create the ankle and knee.

Row 6: Cast (bind) off 1 st, p1 icos, p2tog (hold 2 sts on spare needle for working leg). Rep from beg once more. (4 sts on spare needle in total)

Shape leg

Row 7: With av, cast on 1 st, with RS facing k4 from spare needle of Claws, cast on 1 st. (6 sts)

Work 11 rows st st.

Row 19: Inc, k4, inc. (8 sts)

Work 3 rows st st.

Cast (bind) off.

Right Side of Body

With av, cast on 11 sts.

Row 1: Knit.

Row 2: Cast (bind) off 7 sts, p4 icos, cast on 5 sts. (9 sts)

Row 3: Knit.

Row 4: Cast (bind) off 4 sts, p5 icos, cast on 3 sts. (8 sts)

Row 5: Knit.

Row 6: P2tog, p6, cast on 2 sts. (9 sts)

Row 7: K7, k2tog. (8 sts)

Row 8: P2tog, p6, cast on 2 sts. (9 sts)

Join in te.

Row 9: K7av, k2togte. (8 sts)

Row 10: P2togte, p6av, cast on 2av sts. (9 sts)

Row 11: K5av, k1te, k1av, k2togte. (8 sts)

Row 12: P2togte, p1av, p1te, p4av, cast on 2av sts. (9 sts)

Row 13: K6av, k1te, k1av, k1te.

Row 14: P2togte, p1te, p1av, p1te, p4av, cast on 2av sts. (10 sts)

Row 15: K6av, k1te, k2av, k1te.

Row 16: P2togte, p1av, p1te, p6av, with WS facing p10 from spare needle of Right Back Leg, cast on 2av sts. (21 sts)

Row 17: K15av, k1te, k3av, k2te.

Row 18: P2togte, p4av, p1te, p2av, p1te, p11av, cast on 2av sts. (22 sts)

Row 19: K12av, k1te, k3av, k1te, k3av, k2togte. (21 sts)

Row 20: P2togte, p2av, p1te, p3av, p1te, p12av, cast on 3av sts. (23 sts)

Row 21: K11av, k1te, k2av, k2te, k2av, k2te, k1av, k2togte. (22 sts)

Row 22: Cast (bind) off 3te sts, p1te icos, p2av, p2te, p2av, p2te, p3av, p1te, p6av. (19 sts)

Row 23: Incav, k4av, k1te, k4av, k2te, k2av, k2te, k1av, k2togte. (19 sts)

Row 24: Cast (bind) off 3te sts, p1te icos, p2av, p2te, p4av, p2te, p5av. (16 sts)

Row 25: Incav, k4av, k2te, k3av, k2te, k2av, k2togte. (16 sts)

Row 26: Cast (bind) off 4te sts, p1te icos, p3av, p2te, p6av. (12 sts)

Row 27: K7av, k1te, k2av, k2togte. (11 sts)

Row 28: Cast (bind) off 4te, 3av sts, p4av icos (hold 4 sts on spare needle for Neck and Head).

Left Side of Body

With av, cast on 11 sts.

Row 1: Purl.

Row 2: Cast (bind) off 7 sts, k4 icos, cast on 5 sts. (9 sts)

Row 3: Purl.

Row 4: Cast (bind) off 4 sts, k5 icos, cast on 3 sts. (8 sts)

Row 5: Purl.

Row 6: K2tog, k6, cast on 2 sts. (9 sts)

Row 7: P7, p2tog. (8 sts)

Row 8: K2tog, k6, cast on 2 sts. (9 sts)

Join in te.

Row 9: P7av, p2togte. (8 sts)

Row 10: K2togte, k6av, cast on 2av sts. (9 sts)

Row 11: P5av, p1te, p1av, p2togte. (8 sts)

Row 12: K2togte, k1av, k1te, k4av, cast on 2av sts. (9 sts)

Row 13: P6av, p1te, p1av, p1te.

Row 14: K2togte, k1te, k1av, k1te, k4av, cast on 2av sts. (10 sts)

Row 15: P6av, p1te, p2av, p1te.

Row 16: K2togte, k1av, k1te, k6av, with RS

Teeth

French knots make the teeth for this naughty little dinosaur.

facing k10 from spare needle of Left Back Leg, cast on 2av sts. (21 sts)
Row 17: P15av, p1te, p3av, p2te.
Row 18: K2togte, k4av, k1te, k2av, k1te, k11av, cast on 2av sts. (22 sts)
Row 19: P12av, p1te, p3av, p1te, p3av, p2togte. (21 sts)
Row 20: K2togte, k2av, k1te, k3av, k1te, k12av, cast on 3av sts. (23 sts)
Row 21: P11av, p1te, p2av, p2te, p2av, p2te, p1av, p2togte. (22 sts)
Row 22: Cast (bind) off 3te sts, k1te icos, k2av, k2te, k2av, k2te, k3av, k1te, k6av. (19 sts)
Row 23: Incav, p4av, p1te, p4av, p2te, p2av, p2te, p1av, p2togte. (19 sts)
Row 24: Cast (bind) off 3te sts, k1te icos, k2av, k2te, k4av, k2te, k5av. (16 sts)
Row 25: Incav, p4av, p2te, p3av, p2te, p2av, p2togte. (16 sts)
Row 26: Cast (bind) off 4te sts, k1te icos, k3av, k2te, k6av. (12 sts)
Row 27: P7av, p1te, p2av, p2togte. (11 sts)
Row 28: Cast (bind) off 4te, 3av sts, k4av icos (hold 4 sts on spare needle for Neck and Head).

Neck and Head

Row 1: With av and RS facing, k2, k2tog from spare needle of Right Side of Body, then k2tog, k2 from spare needle of Left Side of Body. (6 sts)
Work 3 rows st st.
Row 5: K2, [inc] twice, k2. (8 sts)
Row 6: Purl.
Row 7: K7, w&t (leave 1 st on left-hand needle unworked).
Row 8: Working top of head on centre 6 sts only, p6, w&t.
Row 9: K6, w&t.
Row 10: P6, w&t.
Rep rows 9–10 once more.
Row 13: K7. (8 sts in total)
Work 7 rows st st.
Row 21: K1, k2tog, k2, k2tog, k1. (6 sts)
Row 22: Purl.
Row 23: K1, [k2tog] twice, k1. (4 sts)
Row 24: Purl.
Cast (bind) off.

Tummy

With st, cast on 2 sts.
Beg with a k row, work 2 rows st st.
Row 3: [Inc] twice. (4 sts)

Row 4: Purl.
Row 5: K1, [inc] twice, k1. (6 sts)
Row 6: Purl.
Row 7: K2, [inc] twice, k2. (8 sts)
Row 8: Purl.
Row 9: K3, [inc] twice, k3. (10 sts)
Work 9 rows st st.
Row 19: K3, [k2tog] twice, k3. (8 sts)
Work 3 rows st st.
Row 23: K2, [k2tog] twice, k2. (6 sts)
Work 5 rows st st.
Row 29: K1, [k2tog] twice, k1. (4 sts)
Work 7 rows st st.
Row 37: [K2tog] twice. (2 sts)
Work 7 rows st st.
Row 45: [Inc] twice. (4 sts)
Row 46: Purl.
Row 47: K1, [inc] twice, k1. (6 sts)
Work 5 rows st st.
Row 53: K1, [k2tog] twice, k1. (4 sts)
Work 3 rows st st.
Row 57: [K2tog] twice. (2 sts)
Work 2 rows st st.
Cast (bind) off.

Jaws

With ra, cast on 2 sts.
Beg with a k row, work 2 rows st st.
Row 3: [Inc] twice. (4 sts)
Work 12 rows st st.
Row 16: Knit.
Beg with a k row, work 13 rows st st.
Cast (bind) off.

To Make Up

SEWING IN ENDS Sew in ends, leaving ends from cast on and cast (bound) off rows for sewing up.
LEGS With WS together, fold each leg in half. Sew up each claw and then main leg on RS.
HEAD AND BODY With WS together, sew along back and around tail to 2cm (¾in) from back of back legs.

TUMMY Sew cast on row of tummy to top of tail 2cm (¾in) from back of back legs, and sew along tummy to head, leaving 4cm (1½in) unsewn at head for jaws. Ease and sew tummy to fit body, leaving a 2.5cm (1in) gap between front and back legs on one side.

JAWS With RS of head (st st side) and WS of jaws (reverse st st side) together, sew together with cast on row to bottom flap of jaws, cast (bound) off row to top of jaws and the knit fold line at the back of the jaws.

STUFFING Pipecleaners are used to stiffen the legs and help bend them into shape. Fold a pipecleaner into a 'U' shape and measure against back two legs. Cut to approximately fit, leaving an extra 2.5cm (1in) at both ends. Fold over the ends. Roll a little stuffing around pipecleaner and slip into body, one end down each back leg. Cut a 13cm (5in) pipecleaner, fold one end over, roll in stuffing and slip into tail. Slip a little stuffing into top of head and a tiny amount into lower jaw. Stuff the body of the Velociraptor, using the end of a knitting needle to ease the stuffing into tail and neck, then sew up the gap. Mould body and back legs into shape.

FRONT LEGS Cut a pipecleaner to fit each front leg, with one end folded over and 2cm (¾in) extra to stick into body. Roll in stuffing and slip into front leg. Push end of pipecleaner into body at seam, 2.5cm (1in) from front of back leg. Sew to body and bend into shape.

EYES With bl, sew 2-loop French knots positioned as in photograph.

TEETH With sn, make approx 17 2-loop French knots on edge of jaws.

Ankylosaurus

Meaning 'fused lizard', the Ankylosaurus was built like an armour-plated tank, with a clubbed tail that is reputed to have been able to break a Tyrannosaurus Rex's leg. Despite – or maybe because of – all its inbuilt weaponry (even its eyelids were armoured), it was a slow-moving vegetarian. Godzilla's arch enemy Anguirus, also known as 'killer of the living' in the 1955 film *Godzilla Raids Again*, was based on the Ankylosaurus.

Ankylosaurus

The Ankylosaurus is fairly complex to knit, due to all his spikes.

Measurements
Length: 30cm (12in)
Height to centre back: 12cm (4¾in)

Materials
Pair of 2¾mm (US 2) knitting needles
Double-pointed 2¾mm (US 2) knitting needles (for i-cord and for holding stitches)
25g (1oz) of Rowan Felted Tweed in Cinnamon 175 (cn)
10g (¼oz) of Rowan Pure Wool 4ply in Porcelaine 451 (po)
20g (¾oz) of Rowan Felted Tweed in Carbon 159 (cb)
Tiny amount of Rowan Pure Wool 4ply in Black 404 (bl) for eyes and claws
2 pipecleaners for legs

Abbreviations
See page 78.
See page 79 for Wrap and Turn Method.
See page 79 for I-cord Technique.

Right Back Leg
With cn, cast on 19 sts.
Row 1: K5, p2, k5, p2, k5.
Row 2: P5, k2, p5, k2, p5.
Row 3: K2tog, k3, p2, k5, p2, k3, k2tog. (17 sts)
Row 4: P4, k2, p5, k2, p4.
Row 5: K2tog, k2, p2, k2tog, k1, k2tog, p2, k2, k2tog. (13 sts)
Row 6: P3, k2, p3, k2, p3.
Row 7: K2tog, k9, k2tog. (11 sts)
Work 3 rows st st.
Row 11: K1, inc, k7, inc, k1. (13 sts)
Work 3 rows st st.
Row 15: K1, inc, k9, inc, k1. (15 sts)
Work 3 rows st st.
Row 19: K1, inc, k11, inc, k1. (17 sts)
Work 3 rows st st.
Row 23: K1, inc, k13, inc, k1. (19 sts)
Row 24: Purl.**
Row 25: K1, inc, k15, inc, k1. (21 sts)
Row 26: Purl.
Row 27: K1, inc, k17, inc, k1. (23 sts)
Row 28: Purl.*
Row 29: Cast (bind) off 11 sts, k to end (hold 12 sts on spare needle for Right Side of Body).

Left Back Leg
Work as for Right Back Leg to *.
Row 29: K12, cast (bind) off 11 sts (hold 12 sts on spare needle for Left Side of Body).

Right Front Leg
Work as for Right Back Leg to **.
Row 25: Cast (bind) off 9 sts, k to end (hold 10 sts on spare needle for Right Side of Body).

Left Front Leg
Work as for Right Back Leg to **.
Row 25: K10, cast (bind) off 9 sts (hold 10 sts on spare needle for Left Side of Body).

Shell
The Ankylosaurus wears his armour-plated shell like a lid on top of his body.

Right Side of Body

With cn, cast on 8 sts.
Row 1: K8, cast on 3 sts. (11 sts)
Row 2: P11, cast on 3 sts. (14 sts)
Row 3: K14, with RS facing k12 from spare needle of Right Back Leg. (26 sts)
Row 4: P26, with WS facing p10 from spare needle of Right Front Leg, cast on 2 sts. (38 sts)
Row 5: Knit.
Row 6: Purl.
Row 7: Inc, k37. (39 sts)
Row 8: Purl.
Row 9: Knit.
Row 10: Cast (bind) off 30 sts, p to end (hold 9 sts on spare needle for Neck and Head).

Left Side of Body

With cn, cast on 8 sts.
Row 1: P8, cast on 3 sts. (11 sts)
Row 2: K11, cast on 3 sts. (14 sts)
Row 3: P14, with WS facing p12 from spare needle of Left Back Leg. (26 sts)
Row 4: K26, with RS facing k10 from spare needle of Left Front Leg, cast on 2 sts. (38 sts)
Row 5: Purl.
Row 6: Knit.
Row 7: Inc, p37. (39 sts)
Row 8: Knit.
Row 9: Purl.
Row 10: Cast (bind) off 30 sts, k to end (hold 9 sts on spare needle for Neck and Head).

Neck and Head

Row 1: With cn and RS facing, k9 from spare needle of Right Side of Body, then k9 from spare needle of Left Side of Body. (18 sts)
Row 2: P8, p2tog, p8. (17 sts)
Row 3: P1, p2tog, p11, p2tog, p1. (15 sts)
Row 4: K1, k2tog, k9, k2tog, k1. (13 sts)
Join in po.
Row 5: K1cn, *k3po, turn.

With double-pointed needles and po, work i-cord on 3 po sts only as folls:
Knit 5 rows.
Next row: K2tog, k1. (2 sts)
Next row: K2tog and fasten off.
With cn, pick up and k3 sts where po meets 3cn sts on row 5*, k5; rep from * to * once more, k1.
Row 6: Purl.
Row 7: K10, w&t (leave 3 sts on left-hand needle unworked).
Row 8: Working on centre 7 sts only, p7, w&t.
Row 9: K7, w&t.
Row 10: K7, p3. (13 sts in total)
Row 11: K3, p7, k3.
Row 12: P1, p2tog, p7, p2tog, p1. (11 sts)
Row 13: Knit.
Row 14: P3, p2tog, p1, p2tog, p3. (9 sts)
Row 15: Knit.
Row 16: P2, p2tog, p1, p2tog, p2. (7 sts)
Row 17: Knit.
Row 18: P1, p2tog, p1, p2tog, p1. (5 sts)
Cast (bind) off.

Tummy

With cn, cast on 3 sts.
Beg with a k row, work 12 rows st st.
Row 13: K1, inc, k1. (4 sts)
Work 9 rows st st.
Row 23: K1, [inc] twice, k1. (6 sts)
Work 7 rows st st.
Row 31: K1, inc, k2, inc, k1. (8 sts)
Work 5 rows st st.
Row 37: K1, inc, k4, inc, k1. (10 sts)
Work 7 rows st st.
Row 45: K1, inc, k6, inc, k1. (12 sts)
Work 9 rows st st.
Row 55: K1, inc, k8, inc, k1. (14 sts)
Work 3 rows st st.
Row 59: K1, inc, k10, inc, k1. (16 sts)
Work 43 rows st st.
Row 103: K2tog, k12, k2tog. (14 sts)
Row 104: Purl.

Row 105: K2tog, k10, k2tog. (12 sts)
Row 106: Purl.
Row 107: K2tog, k8, k2tog. (10 sts)
Row 108: P2tog, k6, p2tog. (8 sts)
Work 4 rows st st.
Row 113: K2tog, k4, k2tog. (6 sts)
Row 114: Purl.
Row 115: K2tog, k2, k2tog. (4 sts)
Row 116: [P2tog] twice. (2 sts)
Row 117: K2tog and fasten off.

Top of Body and Tail
With cb, cast on 3 sts.
Beg with a k row, work 12 rows st st.
Row 13: K1, inc, k1. (4 sts)
Work 9 rows st st.
Row 23: K1, [inc] twice, k1. (6 sts)
Work 7 rows st st.
Row 31: K1, inc, k2, inc, k1. (8 sts)
Work 5 rows st st.
Row 37: K1, inc, k4, inc, k1. (10 sts)
Work 7 rows st st.
Row 45: K1, inc, k6, inc, k1. (12 sts)
Work 9 rows st st.
Row 55: K1, inc, k8, inc, k1. (14 sts)
Work 3 rows st st.
Row 59: K1, inc, k10, inc, k1. (16 sts)
Row 60: P1, inc, p12, inc, p1. (18 sts)
Row 61: K1, inc, k6, inc, k7, inc, k1. (21 sts)
Row 62: P1, inc, p17, inc, p1. (23 sts)
Row 63: Purl.
Row 64: Knit.
Row 65: [P2, k5] 3 times, p2.
Row 66: [K2, p5] 3 times, k2.
Rep rows 65–66 once more.
Join in po.
Row 69: **P2cb, k1cb, k3po, turn.
With double-pointed needles and po,
work i-cord on 3 po sts only as folls:
Knit 3 rows.
Next row: K2tog, k1. (2 sts)
Next row: K2tog and fasten off.
With cb, pick up and k3 sts where you
changed to po on row 69, k1**; rep from ** to

** twice more, p2.
Row 70: Rep row 66.
Row 71: Rep row 65.
Row 72: Rep row 66.
Row 73: Purl.
Row 74: Knit.
Rep rows 65–74 once more.
Rep rows 65–70 once more.
Row 91: [P2tog] twice, p15, [p2tog] twice.
(19 sts)
Row 92: [K2tog] twice, k11, [k2tog] twice.
(15 sts)
Row 93: K2tog, k1, p2, k5, p2, k1, k2tog.
(13 sts)
Row 94: P2tog, k2, p5, k2, p2tog. (11 sts)
Row 95: K2tog, p1, k5, p1, k2tog. (9 sts)
Row 96: K2, p5, k2.
Join in po.
Row 97: P2cb, k1cb, k3po, turn.
With double-pointed needles and po,
work i-cord on 3 po sts only as folls:
Knit 5 rows.
Next row: K2tog, k1. (2 sts)
Next row: K2tog and fasten off,
With cb, pick up and k3 sts where you
changed to po on row 97, k1, p2.
Row 98: K2tog, p5, k2tog. (7 sts)
Row 99: P1, k5, p1.
Row 100: P2tog, p3, p2tog. (5 sts)
Row 101: Purl.
Row 102: Knit.
Cast (bind) off.

End of Tail
With cn, cast on 4 sts.
Row 1: Inc, k2, inc. (6 sts)
Knit 2 rows.
Row 4: Inc, k4, inc. (8 sts)
Knit 3 rows.
Row 8: K2tog, k4, k2tog. (6 sts)
Knit 2 rows.
Row 11: K2tog, k2, k2tog. (4 sts)
Cast (bind) off.

To Make Up

SEWING IN ENDS Sew in ends, leaving ends from cast on and cast (bound) off rows for sewing up.

LEGS With WS together, fold each leg in half and sew up on RS, starting at feet.

TAIL Sew from tip of tail sections to bottom, with end of tail sewn between two (like a sandwich), approx 1cm (½in) from end of tail.

TOP OF BODY Sew top of body so that it sits on top of sides, using running stitch approx 3mm (⅛in) in from the edge. The cast (bound) off row should fit just behind horns on reverse st st row.

TUMMY Sew cast (bind) off row of tummy to nose. Ease and sew tummy to fit body along both sides, leaving a 2.5cm (1in) gap between front and back legs on one side.

STUFFING Pipecleaners are used to stiffen the legs and help bend them into shape. Fold a pipecleaner into a 'U' shape and measure against front two legs. Cut to approximately fit, leaving an extra 2.5cm (1in) at both ends. Fold over the ends. Roll a little stuffing around pipecleaner and slip into body, one end down each front leg. Repeat with second pipecleaner and back legs. Starting at the head, stuff the Ankylosaurus firmly, using the end of a knitting needle to ease the stuffing into tail and neck, then sew up the gap. Mould body into shape.

CLAWS With bl, sew three 4-loop French knots on front of each foot, spaced 4cm (1½in) apart.

EYES With bl, sew 3-loop French knots on reverse st st row, 2 rows in front of the horns.

Brachiosaurus

The Brachiosaurus was unusual in that it had longer front than back legs, hence the name 'arm lizard'. It was a vegetarian and lived in herds. Its head was tiny, representing just one 200th of its body volume. It is unlikely that the Brachiosaurus could rear up on its back legs as depicted in *Jurassic Park*. A life-sized Brachiosaurus skeleton greets airline passengers at O'Hare Airport in Chicago.

Brachiosaurus

The Brachiosaurus is one of the simplest dinosaurs to knit.

Measurements
Length nose to tail: 62cm (24½in)
Height to top of head: 37cm (14½in)

Materials
Pair of 3¾mm (US 5) knitting needles
Double-pointed 3¾mm (US 5) knitting needles (for holding stitches)
45g (1¾oz) of Rowan Felted Tweed Aran in Stoney 742 (st)
Tiny amount of Rowan Pure Wool DK in Black 004 (bl) for eyes
2 tiny black beads for eyes and sewing needle and black thread for sewing on
65cm (25½in) of 3mm armature wire for head, body and tail

Abbreviations
See page 78.

Right Back Leg
With st, cast on 12 sts.
Beg with a k row, work 2 rows st st.
Row 3: K5, k2tog, k5. (11 sts)
Row 4: Purl.
Work 14 rows st st.*
Row 19: Cast (bind) off 5 sts, k to end (hold 6 sts on spare needle for Right Side of Body).

Left Back Leg
Work as for Right Back Leg to *.
Row 19: K6, cast (bind) off 5 sts (hold 6 sts on spare needle for Left Side of Body).

Right Front Leg
Work as for Right Back Leg to *.
Work 4 rows st st.
Row 23: K1, inc, k7, inc, k1. (13 sts)
Row 24: Purl.**
Row 25: Cast (bind) off 6 sts, k to end (hold 7 sts on spare needle for Right Side of Body).

Left Front Leg
Work as for Right Front Leg to **.
Row 25: K7, cast (bind) off 6 sts (hold 7 sts on spare needle for Left Side of Body).

Right Side of Body
With st, cast on 16 sts.
Row 1: Knit.
Row 2: Inc, p14, inc. (18 sts)
Row 3: Knit.
Row 4: Inc, p16, inc, with WS facing p7 from spare needle of Right Front Leg. (27 sts)
Row 5: Knit.
Row 6: P26, inc. (28 sts)
Row 7: Inc, k27, with RS facing k6 from spare needle of Right Back Leg. (35 sts)
Row 8: Purl.
Row 9: Inc, k34, cast on 34 sts. (70 sts)
Row 10: Cast (bind) off 6 sts, p to end. (64 sts)
Row 11: Inc, k63. (65 sts)
Row 12: Cast (bind) off 12 sts, p to end. (53 sts)
Row 13: Inc, k52. (54 sts)
Row 14: Cast (bind) off 12 sts, p to end. (42 sts)
Row 15: Inc, k41. (43 sts)
Row 16: Cast (bind) off 6 sts, p to end. (37 sts)
Row 17: Inc, k36. (38 sts)
Row 18: Cast (bind) off 6 sts, p to end. (32 sts)
Row 19: Inc, k31. (33 sts)
Row 20: Cast (bind) off 10 sts, p to end. (23 sts)

Row 21: Inc, k22. (24 sts)
Row 22: Cast (bind) off 12 sts, p to end. (12 sts)
Row 23: Inc, k11. (13 sts)
Row 24: Cast (bind) off 4 sts, p to end. (9 sts)
Row 25: Inc, k6, k2tog.
Row 26: Purl.
Row 27: Inc, k6, k2tog.
Row 28: P2tog, p7. (8 sts)
Row 29: Inc, k5, k2tog.
Row 30: Purl.
Row 31: Inc, k5, k2tog.
Row 32: Purl.
Row 33: Inc, k5, k2tog.
Row 34: P2tog, p6. (7 sts)
Row 35: Inc, k4, k2tog.
Row 36: Purl.
Row 37: Inc, k4, k2tog.
Row 38: Purl.
Row 39: Inc, k4, k2tog.

Legs

The front legs of the Brachiosaurus are longer than the back legs.

Row 40: Purl.
Row 41: Inc, k4, k2tog.
Row 42: P2tog, p5. (6 sts)
Row 43: Inc, k3, k2tog.
Row 44: Purl.
Row 45: Inc, k3, k2tog.
Row 46: Purl.
Row 47: Inc, k3, k2tog.
Row 48: Purl.
Row 49: Knit.
Row 50: Purl.
Row 51: Inc, k3, k2tog.
Work 3 rows st st.
Row 55: Inc, k3, k2tog.
Row 56: P2tog, p4. (5 sts)
Work 4 rows st st.
Row 61: Inc, k2, k2tog.
Work 3 rows st st.
Row 65: Rep row 61.
Work 3 rows st st.
Row 69: Rep row 61.
Work 3 rows st st.
Row 73: Rep row 61.
Work 4 rows st st.
Row 78: P5, cast on 5 sts. (10 sts)
Row 79: Knit.
Row 80: P2tog, p8. (9 sts)
Row 81: K7, k2tog. (8 sts)
Row 82: Purl.
Row 83: Cast (bind) off 4 sts, k to end. (4 sts)
Row 84: Purl.
Cast (bind) off 4 sts.

Left Side of Body

With st, cast on 16 sts.
Row 1: Purl.
Row 2: Inc, k14, inc. (18 sts)
Row 3: Purl.
Row 4: Inc, k16, inc, with RS facing k7 from spare needle of Left Front Leg. (27 sts)
Row 5: Purl.
Row 6: K26, inc. (28 sts)
Row 7: Inc, p27, with WS facing p6 from spare needle of Left Back Leg. (35 sts)

Row 8: Knit.
Row 9: Inc, p34, cast on 34 sts. (70 sts)
Row 10: Cast (bind) off 6 sts, k to end.
(64 sts)
Row 11: Inc, p63. (65 sts)
Row 12: Cast (bind) off 12 sts, k to end.
(53 sts)
Row 13: Inc, p52. (54 sts)
Row 14: Cast (bind) off 12 sts, k to end.
(42 sts)
Row 15: Inc, p41. (43 sts)
Row 16: Cast (bind) off 6 sts, k to end.
(37 sts)
Row 17: Inc, p36. (38 sts)
Row 18: Cast (bind) off 6 sts, k to end.
(32 sts)
Row 19: Inc, p31. (33 sts)
Row 20: Cast (bind) off 10 sts, k to end.
(23 sts)
Row 21: Inc, p22. (24 sts)
Row 22: Cast (bind) off 12 sts, k to end.
(12 sts)
Row 23: Inc, p11. (13 sts)
Row 24: Cast (bind) off 4 sts, k to end. (9 sts)
Row 25: Inc, p6, p2tog. (9 sts)
Row 26: Knit.
Row 27: Inc, p6, p2tog.
Row 28: K2tog, k7. (8 sts)
Row 29: Inc, p5, p2tog.
Row 30: Knit.
Row 31: Inc, p5, p2tog.
Row 32: Knit.
Row 33: Inc, p5, p2tog.
Row 34: K2tog, k6. (7 sts)
Row 35: Inc, p4, p2tog.
Row 36: Knit.
Row 37: Inc, p4, p2tog.
Row 38: Knit.
Row 39: Inc, p4, p2tog.
Row 40: Knit.
Row 41: Inc, p4, p2tog.
Row 42: K2tog, k5. (6 sts)
Row 43: Inc, p3, p2tog.
Row 44: Knit.

Row 45: Inc, p3, p2tog.
Row 46: Knit.
Row 47: Inc, p3, p2tog.
Work 3 rows st st.
Row 51: Inc, p3, p2tog.
Work 3 rows st st.
Row 55: Inc, p3, p2tog.
Row 56: K2tog, k4. (5 sts)
Work 4 rows st st.
Row 61: Inc, p2, p2tog.
Work 3 rows st st.
Row 65: Rep row 61.
Work 3 rows st st.
Row 69: Rep row 61.
Work 3 rows st st.
Row 73: Rep row 61.
Work 4 rows st st.
Row 78: K5, cast on 5 sts. (10 sts)
Row 79: Purl.
Row 80: K2tog, k8. (9 sts)
Row 81: P7, p2tog. (8 sts)
Row 82: Knit.
Row 83: Cast (bind) off 4 sts, p to end. (4 sts)
Row 84: Knit.
Cast (bind) off.

Tummy
With st, cast on 1 st.
Row 1: Inc. (2 sts)
Row 2: Purl.
Row 3: [Inc] twice. (4 sts)
Row 4: Purl.
Row 5: Inc, k2, inc. (6 sts)
Row 6: Purl.
Work 52 rows st st.
Row 59: K2tog, k2, k2tog. (4 sts)
Row 60: Purl.
Row 61: Knit.
Row 62: Purl.
Row 63: [K2tog] twice. (2 sts)
Row 64: Purl.
Row 65: K2tog and fasten off.

To Make Up

SEWING IN ENDS Sew in ends, leaving ends from cast on and cast (bind) off rows for sewing up.

LEGS With WS together, fold each leg in half and sew up on RS, starting at feet.

HEAD AND BODY Using pliers, bend one end of the armature wire to form a small loop for the head. With WS together, sew up the tail around the other end of the wire, then sew body together along back (over the wire spine) and around head to approx 22cm (9in) down neck and front.

TUMMY Sew cast on row of tummy to where back legs begin, and sew cast (bound) off row to 11cm (4½in) from front legs. Ease and sew tummy to fit body, leaving a 2.5cm (1in) gap between front and back legs on one side.

STUFFING Stuff very firmly. You cannot get stuffing right to the bottom of tail, but stuff the rest of Brachiosaurus very well to help him stand up, then sew up the gap. Mould body into shape.

EYES With bl, sew 2-loop French knots, 1 st down from top of head and 4 sts back from nose. Sew black beads on top of knots.

TOES With bl, sew four 5mm (¼in) vertical sts on front of feet, spaced 1 st apart.

Archaeopteryx

Considered by some to be the first bird on earth, an Archaeopteryx fossil was first discovered in southern Germany in the mid-19th century, and was referred to by Charles Darwin in a subsequent edition of *On the Origin of Species*, contributing to Darwin's theory of evolution. Roughly the size of a crow, the Archaeopteryx is considered to be the link between dinosaurs and birds and, although still under debate, the feeling is that it could fly.

Archaeopteryx

One of our favourites
– it is a little more
complicated to put
together, but easy to knit.

Measurements
Length: 24cm (9½in)
Height to top of head: 14cm (5½in)

Materials
Pair of 3¼mm (US 3) knitting needles
Small amount of Rowan Pure Wool 4ply in
    Black 404 (bl) for legs, claws and eyes
5g (⅛oz) of Rowan Fine Tweed in Leyburn
    383 (le)
10g (¼oz) of Rowan Tweed in Muker 587
    (mk)
10g (¼oz) of Rowan Felted Tweed in Clay
    177 (cl)
5 pipecleaners for tail, legs and wings

Abbreviations
See page 78.
See page 79 for Wrap and Turn Method.

Legs
(make 2 the same)
With bl, cast on 4 sts.
Beg with a k row, work 2 rows st st.
Cont in le.
Work 14 rows st st.
Cont in mk.
Work 6 rows st st.
Row 23: K1, [inc] twice, k1. (6 sts)
Work 3 rows st st.
Row 27: K2, [inc] twice, k2. (8 sts)
Row 28: Purl.

Legs and wings
Shape the legs and wings after
stuffing to get the characteristic
'about to fly' look.

Row 29: K3, [inc] twice, k3. (10 sts)
Work 3 rows st st.
Row 33: K4, [inc] twice, k4. (12 sts)
Row 34: Purl.
Cast (bind) off.

Body and Head

With mk, cast on 4 sts.
Beg with a k row, work 24 rows st st.
Row 25: K1, [inc] twice, k1. (6 sts)
Work 3 rows st st.
Row 29: K2, [inc] twice, k2. (8 sts)
Work 3 rows st st.
Row 33: K2, inc, k2, inc, k2. (10 sts)
Row 34: Purl.
Row 35: K2, inc, k4, inc, k2. (12 sts)
Row 36: Purl.
Row 37: K3, inc, k4, inc, k3. (14 sts)
Row 38: Purl.
Row 39: K4, inc, k4, inc, k4. (16 sts)
Work 3 rows st st.
Row 43: K5, inc, k4, inc, k5. (18 sts)
Row 44: Purl.
Row 45: K5, inc, k6, inc, k5. (20 sts)
Work 7 rows st st.
Row 53: K5, k2tog, k6, k2tog, k5. (18 sts)
Row 54: Purl.
Row 55: K4, k2tog, k6, k2tog, k4. (16 sts)
Row 56: Purl.
Row 57: K4, k2tog, k4, k2tog, k4. (14 sts)
Row 58: Purl.
Row 59: K4, w&t (leave 10 sts on left-hand
needle unworked).
Row 60: Working on 4 sts only, p4.
Row 61: K4, w&t.
Rep rows 60–61 once more.
Row 64: P4.
Row 65: K4, k2tog, k2, k2tog, k4. (12 sts)
Row 66: P4, w&t (leave 8 sts on left-hand
needle unworked).
Row 67: Working on 4 sts only, k4.
Row 68: P4, w&t.
Rep rows 67–68 once more.
Row 71: K4.

Row 72: P3, p2tog, p2, p2tog, p3. (10 sts)
Row 73: K2, k2tog, k2, k2tog, k2. (8 sts)
Work 5 rows st st.
Cont in le.
Work 4 rows st st.
Row 83: K6, w&t (leave 2 sts on left-hand
needle unworked).
Row 84: Working top of head on centre 4 sts
only, p4, w&t.
Row 85: K4, w&t.
Rep rows 84–85 once more.
Row 88: P4, w&t.
Row 89: K6. (8 sts in total)
Row 90: P1, p2tog, p2, p2tog, p1. (6 sts)
Work 3 rows st st.
Row 94: P1, [p2tog] twice, p1. (4 sts)
Work 2 rows st st.
Row 97: [K2tog] twice. (2 sts)
Row 98: P2tog and fasten off.

Tail Feathers

With cl, cast on 2 sts.
Row 1: Knit.
Row 2: Purl.
Row 3: Purl.
Row 4: Knit.
Row 5: Knit.
Row 6: Purl.
Row 7: Purl.
Row 8: Inc, k1. (3 sts)
Row 9: Knit.
Row 10: Purl.
Row 11: Purl.
Row 12: Inc, k2. (4 sts)
Row 13: Knit.
Row 14: Purl.
Row 15: Purl.
Row 16: Knit.
Row 17: Knit.
Row 18: Purl.
Row 19: Purl.
Row 20: Inc, k3. (5 sts)
Row 21: Knit.
Row 22: Purl.

Row 23: Purl.
Row 24: Knit.
Row 25: Knit.
Rep rows 22–25 once more.
Row 30: Purl.
Row 31: Purl.
Row 32: Inc, k4. (6 sts)
Row 33: Knit.
Row 34: Purl.
Row 35: Purl.
Row 36: Knit.
Rep rows 33–36, 5 times more.
Row 57: K2tog, k4. (5 sts)
Row 58: Purl.
Row 59: Purl.
Row 60: Knit.
Row 61: Knit.
Row 62: Purl.
Row 63: Purl.
Row 64: Knit.
Row 65: K2tog, k3. (4 sts)
Row 66: Purl.
Row 67: Purl.
Row 68: Knit.
Row 69: K2tog, k2. (3 sts)
Row 70: Purl.
Row 71: Purl.
Row 72: Knit.
Row 73: Knit.
Row 74: Purl.
Row 75: Purl.
Cast (bind) off.

Wings
(make 2 the same)
With mk, cast on 6 sts.
Beg with a k row, work 4 rows st st.
Row 5: Inc, k4, inc. (8 sts)
Work 11 rows st st.
Row 17: K1, k2tog, k2, k2tog, k1. (6 sts)
Work 3 rows st st.
Row 21: K1, [k2tog] twice, k1. (4 sts)
Row 22: Purl.
Row 23: K1, [inc] twice, k1. (6 sts)

Work 3 rows st st.
Row 27: K1, inc, k2, inc, k1. (8 sts)
Work 5 rows st st.
Row 33: K1, k2tog, k2, k2tog, k1. (6 sts)
Row 34: Purl.
Cast (bind) off.

Wing Feathers
(make 2 the same)
With cl, cast on 4 sts.
Row 1: Knit.
Row 2: Purl.
Row 3: Purl.
Row 4: Knit.
Row 5: Inc, k3. (5 sts)
Row 6: Purl.
Row 7: Inc, p4. (6 sts)
Row 8: Knit.
Row 9: Knit.
Row 10: Purl.
Row 11: Purl.
Row 12: Knit.
Row 13: Inc, k5. (7 sts)
Row 14: Purl.
Row 15: Purl.
Row 16: Knit.
Row 17: Knit.
Rep rows 14–17, 4 times more.
Row 34: Purl.
Row 35: P5, p2tog. (6 sts)
Row 36: Knit.
Row 37: Knit.
Row 38: Purl.
Row 39: P2tog, p4. (5 sts)
Row 40: Knit.
Cast (bind) off.

To Make Up
SEWING IN ENDS Sew in ends, leaving ends from cast on and cast (bound) off rows for sewing up.
LEGS With WS together, fold each leg in half and sew up on RS, starting at feet. Leave open at top of leg.

BODY AND HEAD With WS together, fold body in half and sew around head, body and tail, leaving a 2.5cm (1in) gap.

WINGS With WS together, fold each wing in half and sew together, leaving top open.

STUFFING Pipecleaners are used to stiffen the legs, wings and tail and help bend them into shape. Cut a pipecleaner to approximately fit each leg/wing, leaving an extra 2.5cm (1in) at one end. Fold the end over to stop the pipecleaner poking out of the bottom of the feet/wings. Roll a little stuffing around pipecleaner and slip down each leg/wing. Add some stuffing to top of legs. Leave top of leg/wing open, pipecleaner sticking out. Slip a pipecleaner into the tail and cut off in the body. Stuff the head and body, starting at the beak (no need to stuff the tail), then sew up the gap and mould into shape.

ATTACHING LEGS Push pipecleaner of back leg into the tummy, 4cm (1½in) from tail. Using whip stitch, sew the leg to the tummy. Bend into shape.

ATTACHING WINGS Sew wing feathers to seam of wing. Slip pipecleaner into body 6 sts from seam and above leg. Sew to body and bend into a slight arc.

TAIL FEATHERS Sew tail feathers to tail, starting at top of tail and slightly gathering at tip of tail.

EYES With bl, sew 2-loop French knots positioned as in photograph.

WING CLAWS With bl, make 3 loops at the tip of wing for claws.

Mammoth

A distant relative of the elephant, the Mammoth was hunted by early man for its lovely woolly coat and delicious meat. Humans also frequently drew these creatures on the walls of their caves. The Mammoth's tusks could grow to an enormous 15 feet, but its ears were smaller to conserve heat. Footage was released a few years ago that shows a Mammoth crossing a river in Siberia, so maybe they did not die out 4,000 years ago but are still roaming free in Russia.

Mammoth

The Mammoth is knitted in two mohair blend yarns used together to look woolly.

Measurements
Length: 36cm (14in)
Height to top of head: 25cm (10in)

Materials
Pair of 4mm (US 6) knitting needles
Double-pointed 4mm (US 6) knitting needles (for holding stitches)
Pair of 3¾mm (US 5) knitting needles
80g (3oz) of Rowan Kid Classic in Bitter Sweet 866 (bi)
40g (1½oz) of Rowan Kidsilk Haze in Majestic 589 (ma)
NOTE: most of this animal uses 1 strand of bi and 1 strand of ma held together, and this is called bima
10g (¼oz) of Rowan Creative Focus Worsted in Natural 100 (na)
Tiny amount of Rowan Pure Wool 4ply in Black 404 (bl) for eyes
2 tiny black beads for eyes and sewing needle and black thread for sewing on
80cm (32in) of 3mm armature wire for legs
3 pipecleaners for trunk and tusks

Abbreviations
See page 78.
See page 79 for Wrap and Turn Method.

Toenails
The Mammoth's toenails are embroidered on.

Right Front Leg
With 4mm (US 6) needles and bima, cast on 16 sts.
Beg with a k row, work 26 rows st st.*
Row 27: Cast (bind) off 8 sts, k to end (hold 8 sts on spare needle for Right Side of Body).

Left Front Leg
Work as for Right Front Leg to *.
Row 27: K8, cast (bind) off 8 sts (hold 8 sts on spare needle for Left Side of Body).

Right Back Leg
With 4mm (US 6) needles and bima, cast on 16 sts.
Beg with a k row, work 20 rows st st.
Row 21: K1, inc, k12, inc, k1. (18 sts)
Row 22: Purl.
Row 23: K1, inc, k14, inc, k1. (20 sts)
Row 24: Purl.

Row 25: K1, inc, k16, inc, k1. (22 sts)
Row 26: Purl.
Row 27: K1, inc, k18, inc, k1. (24 sts)
Row 28: Purl.
Row 29: K1, inc, k20, inc, k1. (26 sts)
Row 30: Purl.**
Row 31: Cast (bind) off 13 sts, k to end (hold 13 sts on spare needle for Right Side of Body).

Left Back Leg
Work as Right Back Leg to **.
Row 31: K13, cast (bind) off 13 sts (hold 13 sts on spare needle for Left Side of Body).

Right Side of Body
With 4mm (US 6) needles and bima, cast on 12 sts.
Row 1: Inc, k10, inc. (14 sts)
Row 2: Inc, p12, inc. (16 sts)
Row 3: Inc, k14, inc. (18 sts)
Row 4: Purl.
Break off yarn.
Row 5: With RS facing, rejoin yarn and k8 from spare needle of Right Front Leg, k18 from row 4, then k13 from spare needle of Right Back Leg. (39 sts)
Row 6: P38, inc. (40 sts)
Work 10 rows st st.
Row 17: K38, k2tog. (39 sts)
Row 18: Purl.
Row 19: K37, k2tog. (38 sts)
Row 20: Purl.
Row 21: K36, k2tog. (37 sts)
Row 22: Purl.
Row 23: K35, k2tog. (36 sts)
Row 24: Cast (bind) off 4 sts, p to end. (32 sts)
Row 25: K30, k2tog. (31 sts)
Row 26: Cast (bind) off 4 sts, p to end. (27 sts)
Row 27: K25, k2tog. (26 sts)
Row 28: Cast (bind) off 4 sts, p to end. (22 sts)

Row 29: K20, k2tog. (21 sts)
Row 30: Cast (bind) off 4 sts, p to end. (17 sts)
Row 31: K15, k2tog. (16 sts)
Row 32: P2tog, p to end (hold 15 sts on spare needle for Neck and Head).

Left Side of Body
With 4mm (US 6) needles and bima, cast on 12 sts.
Row 1: Inc, p10, inc. (14 sts)
Row 2: Inc, k12, inc. (16 sts)
Row 3: Inc, p14, inc. (18 sts)
Row 4: Knit.
Break off yarn.
Row 5: With WS facing, rejoin yarn and p8 from spare needle of Left Front Leg, p18 from row 4, then p13 from spare needle of Left Back Leg. (39 sts)
Row 6: K38, inc. (40 sts)
Work 10 rows st st.
Row 17: P38, p2tog. (39 sts)
Row 18: Knit.
Row 19: P37, p2tog. (38 sts)
Row 20: Knit.
Row 21: P36, p2tog. (37 sts)
Row 22: Knit.
Row 23: P35, p2tog. (36 sts)
Row 24: Cast (bind) off 4 sts, k to end. (32 sts)
Row 25: P30, p2tog. (31 sts)
Row 26: Cast (bind) off 4 sts, k to end. (27 sts)
Row 27: P25, p2tog. (26 sts)
Row 28: Cast (bind) off 4 sts, k to end. (22 sts)
Row 29: P20, p2tog. (21 sts)
Row 30: Cast (bind) off 4 sts, k to end. (17 sts)
Row 31: P15, p2tog. (16 sts)
Row 32: K2tog, k to end (hold 15 sts on spare needle for Neck and Head).

Neck and Head

Row 1: With 4mm (US 6) needles and bima, with RS facing k15 from spare needle of Right Side of Body, then k15 from spare needle of Left Side of Body. (30 sts)

Row 2: Purl.

Work 2 rows st st.

Row 5: K22, w&t (leave 8 sts on left-hand needle unworked).

Row 6: Working top of head on centre 14 sts only, p14, w&t.

Row 7: K14, w&t.
Row 8: P14, w&t.
Row 9: K13, w&t.
Row 10: P12, w&t.
Row 11: K11, w&t.
Row 12: P10, w&t.
Row 13: K9, w&t.
Row 14: P8, w&t.
Row 15: K8, w&t.
Row 16: P8, w&t.
Row 17: K8, w&t.
Row 18: P8, w&t.
Row 19: K9, w&t.
Row 20: P10, w&t.
Row 21: K11, w&t.
Row 22: P12, w&t.
Row 23: K13, w&t.
Row 24: P14, w&t.
Row 25: K22. (30 sts in total)

Row 26: [P1, p2tog] twice, p18, [p2tog, p1] twice. (26 sts)

Work 2 rows st st.

Row 29: [K1, k2tog] twice, k14, [k2tog, k1] twice. (22 sts)

Work 7 rows st st.

Row 37: [K1, k2tog] twice, k10, [k2tog, k1] twice. (18 sts)

Work 7 rows st st.

Row 45: K1, k2tog, k12, k2tog, k1. (16 sts)

Work 5 rows st st.

Row 51: K1, k2tog, k10, k2tog, k1. (14 sts)

Work 5 rows st st.

Row 57: K1, k2tog, k8, k2tog, k1. (12 sts)

Work 5 rows st st.

Row 63: K1, k2tog, k6, k2tog, k1. (10 sts)

Work 5 rows st st.

Row 69: K1, k2tog, k4, k2tog, k1. (8 sts)

Work 5 rows st st.

Row 75: K1, k2tog, k2, k2tog, k1. (6 sts)

Work 5 rows st st.

Row 81: K1, [k2tog] twice, k1. (4 sts)

Work 5 rows st st.

Cast (bind) off.

Tummy

With 4mm (US 6) needles and bima, cast on 6 sts.

Beg with a k row, work 98 rows st st.

Row 99: K2tog, k2, k2tog. (4 sts)

Work 41 rows st st.

Row 141: [K2tog] twice. (2 sts)

Row 142: Purl.

Row 143: K2tog and fasten off.

Tusks

(make 2 the same)

With 3¾mm (US 5) needles and bima, cast on 7 sts.

Beg with a k row, work 6 rows reverse st st. Change to na and st st.

Row 7: P3, p2tog, p2. (6 sts)

Work 14 rows st st.

Row 22: K2, k2tog, k2. (5 sts)

Work 13 rows st st.

Row 36: K1, k2tog, k2. (4 sts)

Work 15 rows st st.

Row 52: K1, k2tog, k1. (3 sts)

Work 5 rows st st.

Row 58: K2tog, k1. (2 sts)

Row 59: Purl.

Row 60: K2tog and fasten off.

Ears

(make 2 the same)

With 4mm (US 6) needles and bima, cast on 6 sts.

Work 2 rows moss (seed) st.

Row 3: Inc, moss (seed) st to end. (7 sts)
Row 4: Moss (seed) st.
Row 5: Inc, moss (seed) st to end. (8 sts)
Row 6: Moss (seed) st.
Row 7: Inc, moss (seed) st to end. (9 sts)
Row 8: Inc, moss (seed) st 7, inc. (11 sts)
Row 9: Moss (seed) st.
Row 10: K2tog, moss (seed) st to last 2 sts, k2tog. (9 sts)
Row 11: K2tog, moss (seed) st to last 2 sts, k2tog. (7 sts)

Cast (bind) off.

Tail

With 4mm (US 6) needles and bima, cast on 5 sts.

Beg with a k row, work 3 rows st st.

Row 4: P2tog, p1, p2tog. (3 sts)

Work 10 rows st st.

Row 15: K2tog, k1. (2 sts)

Work 9 rows st st.

Row 25: K2tog and fasten off.

To Make Up

SEWING IN ENDS Sew in ends, leaving ends from cast on and cast (bound) off rows for sewing up.

LEGS With WS together, fold each leg in half and sew up on RS, starting at feet.

HEAD AND BODY With WS together, sew around back and down bottom.

TUMMY AND UNDERSIDE OF TRUNK Sew cast on row of tummy to base of Mammoth's bottom (where legs begin), and sew cast (bound) off row to end of trunk. A pipecleaner is used to bend the trunk into shape. Measure the pipecleaner against the trunk and cut to approximately fit, leaving an extra 2.5cm (1in) at one end. Fold the end over to stop the pipecleaner poking out of the end of the trunk. Roll a little stuffing around pipecleaner and sew up trunk around it. Ease and sew tummy to fit body, leaving an 8cm (3in) gap on one side.

STUFFING Bend the armature wire into a 'U' shape and cut to fit down both front legs, with extra to form a loop for the feet. Use pliers to shape the feet. Roll a little stuffing around wire and slip wire into body, one end down each front leg. Stuff legs firmly. Repeat for back legs. Starting at trunk, stuff body firmly, then sew up gap. Mould body into shape.

TAIL It is not necessary to sew up the tail, as it curls in naturally. Sew tail to back at top of bottom so that tail curls outwards. If necessary, catch it down approx 2cm (¾in) below where you attached it.

EARS Starting at the top, sew cast on row of each ear to side of head, approx 2cm (¾in) down from top of head, with 8 sts between ears and angled slightly towards trunk following w&t line.

TUSKS Cut 14cm (5½in) of pipecleaner and sew up tusk around it, starting at thicker end. Sew tusk to side of head, diagonally just below ear, and sewing bima section with bima and sewing down approx 2cm (¾in) of na. Curl the tusks upwards as in photograph.

EYES With bl, sew 3-loop French knots positioned as in photograph. Sew black beads on top of knots.

TOENAILS With na, sew four 5mm (¼in) vertical lines on front of feet, spaced approx 1.5 sts apart.

Iguanodon

A herbivore from the Cretaceous period, the Iguanodon mainly lived in Europe, including the Isle of Wight, where appropriately we photographed our knitted dinosaurs. Big, bulky and slow-moving, an Iguanodon picks a fight with a Megalosaurus in *Jurassic World*, the fourth of the *Jurassic Park* films. The Iguanodon wins, but only just. The name Iguanodon means 'iguana tooth'.

Iguanodon

The Iguanodon is knitted in tweed yarn to give the impression of scaly skin.

Measurements

Length: 36cm (14in)
Height to top of head: 17cm (6¾in)

Materials

Pair of 3¾mm (US 5) knitting needles
Double-pointed 3¾mm (US 5) knitting
    needles (for holding stitches)
50g (2oz) of Rowan Felted Tweed Aran in
    Dusty 728 (du)
5g (⅛oz) of Rowan Tweed in Burnsall 591
    (bn)
Tiny amount of Rowan Pure Wool 4ply in
    Black 404 (bl) for eyes
2 pipecleaners for legs

Abbreviations

See page 78.
See page 79 for Colour Knitting.
See page 79 for Wrap and Turn Method.

Right Back Leg

First claw

With du, cast on 2 sts.
Row 1: Knit.
Row 2: Purl.
Row 3: [Inc] twice. (4 sts)
Row 4: Cast (bind) off 1 st, p1 icos, p2tog
(hold 2 sts on spare needle for working leg).
Second claw

With du, cast on 2 sts.
Row 1: Knit.
Row 2: Purl.

Row 3: [Inc] twice.** (4 sts)
Row 4: Cast (bind) off 1 st, p1 icos, p2tog,
cast on 3 sts. (5 sts)
Shape leg
Row 5: K5 from Second Claw, with RS facing
k2 from spare needle of First Claw, cast on
3 sts. (10 sts)
Row 6: Purl.
Row 7: K3, [k2tog] twice, k3. (8 sts)
Row 8: Purl.
Row 9: Inc, k1, [k2tog] twice, k1, inc. (8 sts)
Work 7 rows st st.
Row 17: K3, [inc] twice, k3. (10 sts)
Work 3 rows st st.
Row 21: K4, [inc] twice, k4. (12 sts)
Row 22: Purl.*
Row 23: K9, inc, k2. (13 sts)
Row 24: Purl.
Row 25: K9, inc, k3. (14 sts)
Row 26: Purl.
Row 27: Inc, k12, inc. (16 sts)
Work 3 rows st st.
Row 31: Cast (bind) off 7 sts, k to end (hold
9 sts on spare needle for Right Side of Body).

Left Back Leg

Work as for Right Back Leg to *.
Row 23: K2, inc, k9. (13 sts)
Row 24: Purl.
Row 25: K3, inc, k9. (14 sts)
Row 26: Purl.
Row 27: Inc, k12, inc. (16 sts)
Work 3 rows st st.
Row 31: K9, cast (bind) off 7 sts (hold 9 sts
on spare needle for Left Side of Body).

Right Front Leg

Work as for Right Back Leg to **.
Row 4: Cast (bind) off 1 st, p1 icos, p2tog,
cast on 2 sts. (4 sts)
Shape leg
Row 5: K4 from Second Claw, with RS facing
k2 from spare needle of First Claw, cast on
2 sts. (8 sts)

Back and belly

Take the second colour across the back of the knitting using the Fair Isle method and lightly stuff the underbelly.

Row 6: Purl.
Row 7: K2, [k2tog] twice, k2. (6 sts)
Row 8: Purl.
Row 9: Inc, [k2tog] twice, inc. (6 sts)
Work 9 rows st st.
Row 19: Inc, k4, inc. (8 sts)
Work 3 rows st st.
Row 23: K3, [inc] twice, k3. (10 sts)
Row 24: Purl.***
Row 25: Cast (bind) off 5 sts, k to end (hold 5 sts on spare needle for Right Side of Body).

Left Front Leg

Work as for Right Front Leg to ***.
Row 25: K5, cast (bind) off 5 sts (hold 5 sts on spare needle for Left Side of Body).

Right Side of Body

Row 1: With du, cast on 1 st, with RS facing k5 from spare needle of Right Front Leg, cast on 6 sts. (12 sts)
Row 2: Purl.
Row 3: Inc, k11, cast on 2 sts. (15 sts)
Row 4: P15, cast on 2 sts. (17 sts)
Row 5: Inc, k16, cast on 4 sts, with RS facing k9 from spare needle of Right Back Leg, cast on 7 sts. (38 sts)
Join in bn.
Row 6: P33du, p1bn, p3du, incdu. (39 sts)
Row 7: Incdu, k5du, k1bn, k32du, cast on 6du sts. (46 sts)
Row 8: P34du, p1bn, p3du, p1bn, p6du, incdu. (47 sts)
Row 9: Incdu, k6du, k1bn, k4du, k2bn, k33du, cast on 5du sts. (53 sts)
Row 10: P37du, p1bn, p5du, cast (bind) off 2bn, 2du sts, p5du icos, incdu (hold 7 sts on spare needle for Neck and Head).
Row 11: Rejoin du to rem 43 sts, k2togdu, k3du, k1bn, k37du, cast on 5du sts. (47 sts)
Row 12: P40du, p1bn, p2du, p2bn, p2togdu. (46 sts)
Row 13: K2togbn, k4du, k1bn, k23du, k1bn, k5du, k1bn, k9du, cast on 12du sts. (57 sts)
Row 14: Cast (bind) off 8du sts, p12du icos, p1bn, p5du, p1bn, p23du, p2bn, p3du, p2togdu. (48 sts)
Row 15: K2togdu, k2du, k2bn, k3du, k1bn, k11du, k1bn, k7du, k1bn, k6du, k1bn, k11du. (47 sts)
Row 16: Cast (bind) off 8du sts, p3du icos, p2bn, p5du, p1bn, p6du, p2bn, p10du, p1bn, p4du, p2bn, p1du, p2togdu. (38 sts)
Row 17: K2togdu, k1bn, k5du, k1bn, k11du, k1bn, k6du, k1bn, k4du, k2bn, k4du. (37 sts)
Row 18: Cast (bind) off 4du, 2bn, 1du sts, p3du icos, p2bn, p6du, p1bn, p5du, p1bn, p4du, p2bn, p4du, p2togdu. (29 sts)
Row 19: K2togdu, k3du, k2bn, k4du, k2bn, k4du, k1bn, k6du, k2bn, k3du. (28 sts)

Row 20: Cast (bind) off 3du, 2bn sts, p1bn icos, p5du, p1bn, p4du, p1bn, p6du, p2bn, p1du, p2togdu. (22 sts)

Row 21: Cast (bind) off 2du, 1bn sts, k1bn icos, k6du, k1bn, k3du, k2bn, k6du. (19 sts)

Row 22: Cast (bind) off 5du sts, p1du icos, p2bn, p3du, p2bn, p6du. (14 sts)

Row 23: Cast (bind) off 3du sts, k3du icos, k2bn, k3du, k2bn, k1du. (11 sts)

Row 24: Cast (bind off) 1du, 2bn, 3du, 2bn, 3du sts.

Left Side of Body

Row 1: With du, cast on 1 st, with WS facing p5 from spare needle of Left Front Leg, cast on 6 sts. (12 sts)

Row 2: Knit.

Row 3: Inc, p11, cast on 2 sts. (15 sts)

Row 4: K15, cast on 2 sts. (17 sts)

Row 5: Inc, p16, cast on 4 sts, with WS facing p9 from spare needle of Left Back Leg, cast on 7 sts. (38 sts)
Join in bn.

Row 6: K33du, k1bn, k3du, incdu. (39 sts)

Row 7: Incdu, p5du, p1bn, p32du, cast on 6du sts. (46 sts)

Row 8: K34du, k1bn, k3du, k1bn, k6du, incdu. (47 sts)

Row 9: Incdu, p6du, p1bn, p4du, p2bn, p33du, cast on 5du sts. (53 sts)

Row 10: K37du, k1bn, k5du, cast (bind) off 2bn, 2du sts, k5du icos, incdu (hold 7 sts on spare needle for Neck and Head).

Row 11: Rejoin du to rem 43 sts, p2togdu, p3du, p1bn, p37du, cast on 5du sts. (47 sts)

Row 12: K40du, k1bn, k2du, k2bn, k2togdu. (46 sts)

Row 13: P2togbn, p4du, p1bn, p23du, p1bn, p5du, p1bn, p9du, cast on 12du sts. (57 sts)

Row 14: Cast (bind) off 8du sts, k12du icos, k1bn, k5du, k1bn, k23du, k2bn, k3du, k2togdu. (48 sts)

Row 15: P2togdu, p2du, p2bn, p3du, p1bn, p11du, p1bn, p7du, p1bn, p6du, p1bn,

p11du. (47 sts)

Row 16: Cast (bind) off 8du sts, k3du icos, k2bn, k5du, k1bn, k6du, k2bn, k10du, k1bn, k4du, k2bn, k1du, k2togdu. (38 sts)

Row 17: P2togdu, p1bn, p5du, p1bn, p11du, p1bn, p6du, p1bn, p4du, p2bn, p4du. (37 sts)

Row 18: Cast (bind) off 4du, 2bn, 1du sts, k3du icos, k2bn, k6du, k1bn, k5du, k1bn, k4du, k2bn, k4du, k2togdu. (29 sts)

Row 19: P2togdu, p3du, p2bn, p4du, p2bn, p4du, p1bn, p6du, p2bn, p3du. (28 sts)

Row 20: Cast (bind) off 3du, 2bn sts, k1bn icos, k5du, k1bn, k4du, k1bn, k6du, k2bn, k1du, k2togdu. (22 sts)

Row 21: Cast (bind) off 2du, 1bn sts, p1bn icos, p6du, p1bn, p3du, p2bn, p6du. (19 sts)

Row 22: Cast (bind) off 5du sts, k1du icos, k2bn, k3du, k2bn, k6du. (14 sts)

Row 23: Cast (bind) off 3du sts, p3du icos, p2bn, p3du, p2bn, p1du. (11 sts)

Row 24: Cast (bind off) 1du, 2bn, 3du, 2bn, 3du sts.

Neck and Head

Row 1: With du and RS facing, k5, k2tog from spare needle of Right Side of Body, then k2tog, k5 from spare needle of Left Side of Body. (12 sts)

Row 2: Purl.

Row 3: K2tog, k8, k2tog. (10 sts)
Work 3 rows st st.

Row 7: K7, w&t (leave 3 sts on left-hand needle unworked).

Row 8: Working top of head on centre 4 sts only, p4, w&t.

Row 9: K4, w&t.

Row 10: P4, w&t.

Row 11: K4, w&t.

Row 12: P4, w&t.

Row 13: K7. (10 sts in total)

Row 14: P2, p2tog, p2, p2tog, p2. (8 sts)
Work 5 rows st st.

Row 20: P1, p2tog, p2, p2tog, p1. (6 sts)

Row 21: Knit.

Row 22: P1, inc, p2, inc, p1. (8 sts)

Row 23: K1, k2tog, k2, k2tog, k1. (6 sts)
Cast (bind) off.

Tummy

First side

With du, cast on 4 sts.

Row 1: Knit.

Row 2: P4, cast on 3 sts. (7 sts)

Row 3: Knit.

Row 4: P6, inc (hold 8 sts on spare needle).

Second side

With du, cast on 4 sts.

Row 1: Knit.

Row 2: Purl.

Row 3: K4, cast on 3 sts. (7 sts)

Row 4: Purl.

Row 5: With RS facing, k7 from Second Side, then p1, k7 from spare needle of First Side. (15 sts)

Row 6: P7, k1, p7.

Row 7: Inc, k6, p1, k6, inc. (17 sts)

Row 8: P8, k1, p8.

Row 9: K8, p1, k8.
Rep rows 8–9, 7 times more.

Row 24: P2tog, p6, k1, p6, p2tog. (15 sts)

Row 25: K7, p1, k7.

Row 26: P7, k1, p7.
Rep rows 25–26 once more.

Row 29: K2tog, k5, p1, k5, k2tog. (13 sts)

Row 30: P6, k1, p6.

Row 31: K6, p1, k6.
Rep rows 30–31 once more.

Row 34: P2tog, p4, k1, p4, p2tog. (11 sts)

Row 35: K5, p1, k5.

Row 36: P5, k1, p5.

Row 37: K2tog, k3, p1, k3, k2tog. (9 sts)

Row 38: P4, k1, p4.

Row 39: K4, p1, k4.

Row 40: P2, p2tog, k1, p2tog, p2. (7 sts)

Row 41: K3, p1, k3.

Row 42: P3, k1, p3.
Rep rows 41–42 twice more.

Row 47: K1, k2tog, p1, k2tog, k1. (5 sts)
Row 48: P2, k1, p2.
Row 49: K2tog, p1, k2tog. (3 sts)
Row 50: P3tog and fasten off.

To Make Up

SEWING IN ENDS Sew in ends, leaving ends
from cast on and cast (bound) off rows for
sewing up.

LEGS With WS together, fold each leg in
half. Sew up each claw and then main leg
on RS.

HEAD AND BODY With WS together and
starting 2.5cm (1in) from front of front legs,
sew around head, along back and around
tail to 4cm (1½in) from back of back leg.

TUMMY With RS together, fold tummy in
half along reverse st st centre line and sew
along cast on row. With RS of body (st st
side) and WS of tummy (reverse st st side)
together, sew cast on row of tummy to top of
tail, and sew cast (bound) off row to front of
front legs. Ease and sew tummy to fit body,
leaving a 2.5cm (1in) gap between front and
back legs on one side.

STUFFING Pipecleaners are used to stiffen
the legs and help bend them into shape.
Fold a pipecleaner into a 'U' shape and
measure against front two legs. Cut to
approximately fit, leaving an extra 2.5cm
(1in) at both ends. Fold over the ends.
Roll a little stuffing around pipecleaner
and slip into body, one end down each
front leg. Repeat with second pipecleaner
and back legs. Starting at the head, stuff
the Iguanodon firmly, using the end of a
knitting needle to ease the stuffing into tail
and neck, then sew up the gap. Mould body
into shape.

EYES With bl, sew 3-loop French knots
8 rows from nose and 3 sts apart, positioned
as in photograph.

Index of Dinosaurs

Methods

Abbreviations

alt alternate
approx approximately
beg begin(ning)
cm centimetres
cont continue
foll(s) follow(s)(ing)
g grams
icos including cast (bound) off stitch. After casting (binding) off the stated number of stitches, one stitch remains on the right-hand needle. This stitch is included in the number of the following group of stitches
in inches
inc work into front and back of next stitch to increase by one stitch
k knit
k2(3)tog knit next two (three) stitches together
oz ounces
p purl
p2(3)tog purl next two (three) stitches together
rem remain(ing)
rep repeat
RS right side
st(s) stitch(es)
st st stocking (stockinette) stitch
w&t wrap and turn. See Wrap and Turn Method, right.
WS wrong side
[ ] work instructions within square brackets as directed
* work instructions after asterisk(s) as directed

Choosing Yarns

We recommend Rowan Yarns, but as each dinosaur takes only a small amount of yarn, any yarn can be used, either different colours or thicknesses. If using thicker yarns, use needles that are at least two sizes smaller than recommended on the ball band as the tension (gauge) needs to be tight so the stuffing doesn't show. If using thicker yarn and larger needles, your dinosaur will be considerably bigger.

Body and Head

When holding stitches to use later on in the pattern, work the last row on a spare double-pointed needle. This means you can pick up and knit or purl the stitches from either end of the needle.

Carefully follow the instructions when picking up and knitting the first row of Neck and Head. The right side of the body is knitted first, then the left side. The backbone of the dinosaur is in the middle of this row. If picked up incorrectly the head will be facing towards the tail.

Holes can develop around the short-row shaping at the top of the head, and at the nape of the neck after you have sewn up the back of the dinosaur. To solve, Swiss darn over the holes. Swiss darning can also be used to cover up any untidy stitches.

Stuffing

Stuffing the dinosaur is as important as the actual knitting. Use a knitting needle point to push the stuffing into the feet/claws, and into the nose of the dinosaur. Even after the dinosaur is sewn up you can manipulate the stuffing with a knitting needle. If the stitches are distorted you have overstuffed.

An Important Note

The dinosaurs aren't toys, but if you intend to give them to small children do not use pipecleaners in the construction. Instead, you will need to densely stuff the legs to make the dinosaur stand up.

Wrapping Pipecleaners

This method is used for the Pterodactyl. If possible, use coloured pipecleaners and try to match the colour of the wrapping yarn. Leaving a 5cm (2in) tail of free yarn, tightly wrap the yarn around the pipecleaner, making sure no pipecleaner chenille pokes through. Wrap down the pipecleaner to as close to the tip as possible, then wrap the yarn back up to the top. Knot the two ends and slip them into the body. If a little bit of white pipecleaner chenille shows through, colour it in with a matching felt-tip pen. A little dab of clear glue will stop the wrapping from slipping off the end of the pipecleaner.

I-cord Technique

With double-pointed needles, *knit a row. Slide the stitches to the other end of the needle. Do not turn the knitting. Repeat from *, pulling the yarn tight on the first stitch so that the knitting forms a tube.

Wrap and Turn Method

Knit the number of stitches in the first short row. Slip the next stitch purlwise from the left-hand to the right-hand needle. Bring the yarn forward then slip the stitch back onto the left-hand needle. Return the yarn to the back. On a purl row use the same method, taking the yarn back then forward.

Colour Knitting

There are two main techniques for working with more than one colour in the same row of knitting: the intarsia technique and the Fair Isle technique. Most of the dinosaurs use either Fair Isle or intarsia.

Intarsia Technique

This method is used when knitting individual, large blocks of colour. It is best to use a small ball (or long length) for each area of colour, otherwise the yarns will easily become tangled. When changing to a new colour, twist the yarns on the wrong side of the work to prevent holes from forming. When starting a new row, turn the knitting so that the yarns that are hanging from it untwist as much as possible. If you have several colours, you may occasionally have to reorganise the yarns at the back of the knitting. Your work may look messy, but once the ends are all sewn in it will look fine.

Fair Isle (or Stranding) Technique

If there are no more than four stitches between colours you can use the Fair Isle technique. Begin knitting with the first colour, then drop this when you introduce the second colour. When you come to the first colour again, take it under the second colour to twist the yarns. When you come to the second colour again, take it over the first colour. The secret is not to pull the strands on the wrong side of the work too tightly or the work will pucker.

Resources

All the dinosaurs are knitted in Rowan Yarns; for stockists please refer to the Rowan website: www.knitrowan.com. By the time this book is printed some colours may have been discontinued; John Lewis department stores stock Rowan yarns, and will happily suggest alternative colours.

We recommend using 100 per cent polyester or kapok stuffing, available from craft shops and online retailers. A dinosaur takes 20g–80g (¾–3oz) of stuffing, depending on size.

Armature wire is useful for the longer-necked dinosaurs. It is pliable and available from local art shops or on eBay.

We are selling knitting kits for some of the dinosaurs. The kits are packaged in a *Best in Show* knitting bag and contain yarn, all needles required, stuffing, pipecleaners and a pattern.

For those who cannot knit but would like a dinosaur, we are selling some of the dinosaurs ready-made. You can see the dinosaurs on our website: www.muirandosborne.co.uk.

Acknowledgements

Thank you once again to the wonderful group of people who have worked on this book. To Katie Cowan, Amy Christian and Zoë Anspach for their support, yet again, and for knowing much more about dinosaurs than we did. To Marilyn Wilson for her tactful and sensitive as well as eagle-eyed pattern-checking, and to Michelle Pickering for editing the book into shape. Particular thanks go to Holly Jolliffe, for doing it again – wonderful photographs on a freezing cold day, with good humour and brilliance.

Thank you to the Botanic Gardens at Ventnor (www.botanic.co.uk) for letting us use them as a prehistoric backdrop, and to Tom Holland, dinosaur expert among other things, for kindly advising us.

Thank you also to Rowan Yarns yet again for their support, and thank you to our families for encouragement and to the makers of *Broadchurch* and *The Fall* for keeping us entertained, in a grisly kind of way.

The Authors

Sally Muir and Joanna Osborne run their own knitwear business, Muir and Osborne. They export their knitwear to stores in the United States, Japan and Europe as well as selling to shops in the United Kingdom. Several pieces of their knitwear are in the permanent collection at the Victoria and Albert Museum, London. They are the authors of the bestselling *Best in Show: Knit your own Dog*, *Best in Show: 25 More Dogs to Knit*, *Best in Show: Knit your own Cat*, *Knit your own Zoo*, *Knit your own Pet* and *Knit your own Farm*.